*Treasured Recipes
from
Early New England Kitchens*

Treasured Recipes from Early New England Kitchens

MARJORIE PAGE BLANCHARD

Illustrated by
CAROLE COLE GOLDSBOROUGH

GARDEN WAY PUBLISHING
Charlotte, Vermont

Published in association with Harrington's of Richmond, Vermont, Inc.

All rights reserved — no part of this book may be reproduced in any form without permission in writing from the publisher, except by reviewer who wishes to quote brief passages in connection with a review written for inclusion in magazine or newspaper.

Library of Congress Catalog Card Number: 75-23859

ISBN 0-88266-078-0

Copyright 1975 by Harrington's In Vermont, Inc.
Richmond, Vt. 05477

Printed in the United States

The book design is by Irving Perkins. Illustrated by Carole Goldsborough. Cover Design by Morris Gittleson. Front cover of farmhouse kitchen, Stowe, Vermont by Otto Fenn, Courtesy Curtis Publishing Company. Printed by George Little Press.

Foreword

THIS collection of early New England recipes is presented by two New England firms, different in purpose but closely allied in a fundamental way. Both believe strongly in the basic virtues that are part of our heritage: honesty, integrity, thrift, simplicity and a wonderful ability to make do.

For more than 100 years Harrington's has provided the housewife with foods that are a basic part of the New England diet—ham, sausage, bacon, cheese, maple syrup. In more recent years Harrington's has also offered helpful information on how to use these foods in imaginative ways.

Garden Way Publishing is part of a larger organization dedicated to providing dependable equipment and know-how for those who are concerned about the problems of food and resource shortages and environmental conservation, and who are trying to do something about them.

Harrington's, providing quality foods, and Garden Way Publishing, providing sound information on growing and preparing foods—it was natural that the two would work together to explore how our ancestors created wholesome, delicious dishes from what was available.

To compile this collection, with authenticity uppermost in importance, we enlisted the help of Marjorie Blanchard, an author who has researched the subject of colonial New England food and is presenting it to you in the form of a diary, feeling that a bit of background and anecdotal comment will help us understand and make good use of these recipes that are so much a part of our heritage.

Introduction

MY great-grandmother, Agnes Pettigrew, was not only a prolific correspondent, she was a collector and saver, habits no longer practiced in today's living. Perhaps this was due in part to her thrifty Scottish nature, but she also had a great interest in what was going on around her, in her world of travel, family, and friends. She believed in getting out to see at first hand what life was like in other parts of the country, and as she had relatives all over New England, there was always an excuse for a visit. The letters, diaries, and accounts of our ancestors that we have inherited are important. Unfortunately, it is too easy today to pick up the telephone, and our great-grandchildren will have no permanent written records of the daily lives we are leading. Will they have the fun of reading something like the following, from a diary written by a young girl in 1819? "January —. Picked geese in the morning. Washed, pared apples. Set corner biscuits. Went to church half a day. Visited at Mr. Timothy Richards, a large party with an elaborate table. February —. Ironed and washed floor. Count that day lost."

This was one of the first things I found when going through boxes of papers in the attic of the old house that had been in the family for many generations. It was one of those situations that happens to all of us at some time: a trip to the attic to look for one specific item and two hours later I was immersed in reading old letters, my original errand forgotten. I realized that these findings were a part of my heritage and my children's — a link with the past that should not be destroyed. Besides, my curiosity was piqued and I wanted to know just what corner biscuits were, and how that goose was cooked. A bit more searching produced the biscuit recipe, or receipt, and enough comment on the roasting of a goose that I managed to piece together a respectable recipe.

Corner Biscuits

½ cup lukewarm water
2 packages dry yeast
1 tablespoon sugar
4 to 5 cups flour
1 teaspoon nutmeg
2 teaspoons salt
1½ cups buttermilk, lukewarm
½ cup softened butter
2 tablespoons dry sherry

Stir yeast and sugar into lukewarm water. Let stand for 5 minutes until bubbly.

Into large bowl put 4 cups flour, nutmeg, salt, and buttermilk. Mix together. Add yeast and sherry and stir well.

Beat in butter in four pieces.

Turn dough out onto floured board and knead in remaining flour until dough is smooth and no longer sticky. When dough has been kneaded enough it will have blisters, somewhat like moon craters, on its surface.

Put ball of dough in greased bowl and cover. Let rise in a warm place until double in bulk, 1 to 1½ hours.

Punch dough down and with a rolling pin roll it out to ¾ inch thickness. With a 2 inch biscuit cutter, cut circles and place close together in greased baking pans. Cover and let rise 20 to 30 minutes.

Preheat oven to 400°.

Brush tops of biscuits with melted butter. Bake for 15 minutes until golden.

30 BISCUITS

Roast Goose

9 to 10 pound goose
3 fresh sage leaves or 1 tablespoon crumbled dried sage
2 onions, cut up
1 teaspoon salt
Freshly ground pepper
1 cup apple cider

Preheat oven to 375°.
Wash goose and wipe dry. Sprinkle sage, onions, salt, and pepper in cavity. Place goose breast side down on rack in roasting pan. Pour cider in bottom of pan. Roast 15 minutes per pound.
During cooking period, baste several times with cider and prick skin to release fat. Turn breast side up for last half hour of cooking.
Serve with Sauce for Goose.

8 SERVINGS

Sauce for Goose

6 apples, peeled, cored, and quartered
¼ cup white wine
½ teaspoon nutmeg
Grated rind of ½ lemon
1 tablespoon butter
2 tablespoons brandy
¼ cup sugar

Put apples in saucepan with white wine. Cover. Simmer until very soft.
Add nutmeg, lemon rind, butter, and brandy, and mash with fork. Stir in sugar. Serve warm.

Our dinner that night was a feast for an odd Tuesday, but much appreciated, and it started me on a quest for more background on the dining habits of our ancestors. The menus varied with location and, as Rhode Islanders were enjoying jonnycake made from their special white corn meal, the citizens of Massachusetts breakfasted on baked beans and brown bread, and Mainites pulled lobster pots for stews and chowders.

After the first hard years of wretched housing and near starvation, life became much improved in the colonies and, while Yankees were a hardy lot who could live simply and frugally, they were not so far removed from their native lands that they did not indulge themselves in luxuries when the opportunity arose. Trade with England and other countries brought in their spices, tea, coffee, wines, etc., and, while waiting for supplies, the resident colonists could always fall back on venison, wild birds, lobsters of "an enormous size," and a wide variety of fruits and vegetables that grew prolifically in this fertile soil.

After many hours of perusing and sorting old manuscripts, I had a collection of recipes. The basic foods the colonists had to work with varied with geographic areas. Coastal fare was similar from Connecticut to Maine, and inland sections had their similarities too. But each state had its specialties and I have organized the recipes by states, beginning with Connecticut.

Clam Pie • 20
Clam Fritters • 20
Boiled Chicken with Oyster Sauce • 13
Fried Chicken or Turkey • 14
Six Layer Dinner • 21
Scalloped Onions • 18
Onion Shortcake • 18
Buckwheat Cakes • 25
Pumpkin Bread • 15
Pumpkin Pudding • 16
Scorched Cream • 16
Connecticut Peach Pudding • 22
Hedgehog Pudding • 23
Plum Cake • 24

A DIARY written by two sisters in 1801 records in delightful fashion the late teen years of two girls who must have been daughters of one of our wealthier government officials. They take note of "an elegant supper given at the home of the governor with the table set with a great deal of glass and a large pyramid in the center. There was a boiled turkey with sauce of oysters, roast partridges, a variety of birds, tongues, a great quantity of pies, especially pumpkin of which we in Connecticut are especially fond, puddings, etc."

The recipe for oyster sauce for boiled turkey turns up in a couple of old cookbooks and we know that New Haven was justly famous in the Connecticut Colony for its oysters, so the dish was probably seen frequently on the banquet circuit.

The idea of boiling a turkey is at first not appealing as we are so used to the sight of a golden-crisp brown-skinned bird, but the meat is wonderfully moist, even the breast, and remains so for use later. Try a large chicken if you don't want to commit yourself to boiling a whole turkey. Pour the oyster sauce over the bird and garnish liberally with parsley.

Boiled Chicken with Oyster Sauce

4 to 5 pound chicken
Flour
1 pint oysters, drained (reserve liquor)
2 cups bread crumbs
Salt to taste
Freshly ground pepper
½ teaspoon nutmeg
1 cup light cream
1 tablespoon butter mixed with 1 tablespoon flour
Juice of ½ lemon
Parsley sprigs

Dredge chicken with flour. Put in large kettle and cover with lukewarm water. Cover.

Put on high heat and bring to a boil, skimming frequently. When boiling, turn heat to simmer and cook for 15 minutes per pound. When time is up, remove from heat and let stand in broth for 20 minutes.

Meanwhile, chop finely 1 cup oysters and mix with bread crumbs, salt, pepper, and nutmeg. Chill.

Put oyster liquor and cream in saucepan and heat. Stir in butter-flour mixture until thickened. Add remaining oysters and cook for 5 minutes. Add lemon juice and keep warm or reheat without boiling.

Make walnut-sized balls of oyster-crumb mixture. Half fill a saucepan with chicken broth and bring to a boil. Drop in forcemeat balls, a few at a time, and simmer until they float to the top. Remove to platter and keep warm.

When ready to serve, place chicken on platter, surround with forcemeat balls and parsley. Pour some sauce over bird and serve remainder in a sauceboat. For extra color, garnish with sauteed carrots.

6 SERVINGS

The boiling of poultry, any kind, was common and led to the creation of such dishes as the following, which is an old recipe from a famous wayside tavern.

Fried Chicken

Cut ½ inch thick slices from the breast of a boiled chicken or turkey. Heat butter in a large skillet and, over medium heat, saute slices until golden brown on each side. Be generous with the butter and cook slowly. Cut more slices than you think you will need as they will shrink in cooking.

Another feature of Connecticut cuisine was pumpkin in many forms — inspiration for the following lament:

We have pumpkins at morning and pumpkins at noon
If it were not for pumpkins we should be undone.

A famous and excellent recipe that has been handed down since the days of General Israel Putnam is for pumpkin bread. The pumpkin was first cooked in an iron kettle, mixed into dough, settled in an iron crock overnight, then spooned into a pan to bake. Somehow, our modern baking methods are easier and certainly more reliable.

Pumpkin Bread

- 1½ cups mashed, cooked pumpkin
- 4 tablespoons lard or butter
- 4 tablespoons molasses
- 2 teaspoons salt
- 1 cup milk
- 2 packages dry yeast
- 1 cup lukewarm water
- 8 to 9 cups unbleached white flour

In large bowl put pumpkin, lard, molasses, and salt. Scald milk and pour into bowl. Let stand until lukewarm.

Dissolve yeast in lukewarm water and let stand until bubbly. Stir into pumpkin mixture.

Beat in 7 cups flour.

Turn dough onto floured board and knead, adding flour, until dough is no longer sticky. The amount of flour will vary according to the weather (use less on a dry day) and the moisture in the pumpkin. Knead for at least 10 minutes. The dough is ready when it is smooth and has a blistered surface.

Put in greased bowl and cover. Let rise until double in bulk — about 2 hours.

Punch down. Let rise again, covered, until double.

Punch down and shape into 4 loaves for greased 8 x 5 inch pans. Place dough in pans. Cover and let rise until dough almost reaches tops of pans.

Preheat oven to 350°.

Bake bread for 45 to 50 minutes. Turn out and cool on racks.

YIELD: 4 LOAVES

Pumpkin Pudding

¼ cup butter or margarine
½ cup maple syrup
½ teaspoon cinnamon
½ teaspoon mace

3 eggs
1 cup mashed, cooked pumpkin
2 tablespoons amber or dark rum
Whipped cream

Preheat oven to 350°.

Cream butter and maple syrup together. Beat in spices. Blend in eggs and pumpkin, mixing well. Stir in rum.

Pour into buttered 1½ quart baking dish. Bake for 40 minutes until puffy and set.

Serve warm with whipped cream.

6 SERVINGS

Another dish that crops up in the Putnam family records but is also found in cookbooks of the early nineteenth century, is Scorched Cream. Described as a rich custard with a layer of sugar on top, the "scorching" done with a flatiron, it does sound like that well-known English dessert with the French title, Creme Brulee. However, in this case the custard is covered with a meringue, then sprinkled with sugar, then broiled. Actually, this turns out to be somewhat easier than carmelizing and, in a thrifty Yankee way, uses some of the egg whites as well.

Scorched Cream

5 eggs, separated
⅓ cup plus 4 tablespoons sugar
2 cups rich milk

8 very thin slices pound or sponge cake
¼ cup red raspberry or currant jelly

Put yolks and whites into separate bowls.

Beat yolks until light, gradually adding ⅓ cup sugar. Scald milk and pour over yolks while beating.

Pour mixture into saucepan and cook over medium heat, stirring constantly, until thick and smooth.

Pour into bowl. Cover with plastic wrap and chill for 2 hours.

In bottom of shallow 1½ quart baking dish arrange cake slices.

Beat egg whites until stiff but not dry, gradually adding 2 tablespoons sugar.

Spoon custard over cake. Cover completely with meringue. Sprinkle remaining 2 tablespoons sugar over top.

Put under broiler briefly to brown. Watch carefully as it will burn quickly.

Before serving, decorate top with dabs of red jelly.

6 SERVINGS

Connecticut was largely a farm state until the 1850's and was known as the "Provision State" during the Revolution because it provided a great quantity of food to the Colonial Army. The land was rich and there was much traffic on the Connecticut River as sailing barges hauled loads of vegetables down the waterway, out onto Long Island Sound, and on to New York for marketing. Looking through old inventories, I couldn't help but notice the different varieties of onions that were grown, including one called Southport Globe that we can still buy for planting today. One wonders why we are now reduced to a choice of only two or three varieties in our present markets. A diary notes: "October 14 — spent day sorting and stringing onions."

They seemed to do more interesting things with their onions than we do today, creating whole dishes from the vegetable, not just using it for flavoring. Of course their vegetable supply in the winter was limited to what could be wintered over without spoiling and, with no little frozen boxes to choose from, a bit of ingenuity was needed. Scalloped Onions and Onion Shortcake seem indicative of what was provided to accompany the roast game or leg of mutton for the main meal of the day, always served at noon.

Scalloped Onions

6 large onions
4 large plain crackers
Salt to taste
Freshly ground pepper
½ teaspoon grated nutmeg
2 tablespoons butter or margarine
3 cups rich milk or half and half, heated

Preheat oven to 375°.
Peel onions and slice into rings. Put in saucepan and barely cover with water. Boil for 10 minutes. Drain well.
Roll crackers into coarse crumbs.
Butter a shallow 1½ quart baking dish.
Arrange onions and crackers in alternate layers, dotting each layer with butter and sprinkling with salt, pepper, and nutmeg. Pour milk over all.
Bake for 30 minutes.

4 SERVINGS

Onion Shortcake

1 cup flour
2 teaspoons baking powder
1 teaspoon salt
3 tablespoons butter
¼ to ⅓ cup buttermilk
3 cups sliced onions
½ cup sour cream
1 egg
Salt to taste
Freshly ground pepper
½ teaspoon mace

In bowl put flour, baking powder, and salt. Work in butter with fingertips until mixture resembles coarse meal. Pour in buttermilk gradually, mixing until a somewhat sticky dough is formed.

Turn out onto floured board and knead briefly until smooth. Pat dough into a round or rectangular shape ½ inch thick and fit into baking pan.

Put onions in saucepan and barely cover with water. Bring to a boil and cook until soft but not mushy. Drain well.

Preheat oven to 400°.

Place onions over dough, covering it completely. Beat egg with sour cream and seasonings. Pour over onions.

Bake for 20 to 30 minutes, until set.

4 TO 5 SERVINGS

One fascinating bit of old paper that I stumbled upon was a coach schedule listing the stops between New York and Boston. The schedule contained faded notations and comments upon the travel and also on the taverns that were visited along the way. Taverns were so absolutely essential to the traveler that the towns on the route were required by law to have them so the weary human beings who rode the bumpy Post Road would have a place to rest their bruised bones before climbing onto the coach for the rest of the journey. Some taverns were renowned for their food and drink; others not so, as one notation makes clear: "Food very poor in quality and quantity. Landlord stingy with drink." The Morehouse Tavern in Greens Farms, a regular way-stop, served excellent fare with a menu offering a choice of "clam pie or fritters, small roast birds and syllabubs, pies and puddings." The Clam Pie recipe turned up in a very old recipe book from Long Island, which maintained close relations with Connecticut in colonial days. After trying three versions, I came up with this one. It is most economical and very good.

Clam Pie

2 nine ounce cans or 1 pint clams, drained (reserve juice)
4 slices bacon, chopped
1 onion, chopped
½ medium green pepper, chopped
2 medium potatoes, peeled and diced
2 carrots, peeled and diced
2 tablespoons chopped parsley
1 egg
Salt to taste
Freshly ground pepper
Pastry for top crust

Preheat oven to 400°.
Chop bacon and fry until done but not crisp. Remove and drain.
In remaining fat, saute onion and green pepper until soft.
Add potatoes and carrots. Stir all together. Cover pan, turn heat to low, and simmer for 10 minutes.
In 8 inch pie pan put half of vegetables. Cover with half of clams. Repeat layers. Put bacon on top. Sprinkle with parsley.
Beat egg with reserved clam juice and seasonings. Pour over all.
Roll out top crust and fit over pan, crimping edges.
Bake for 25 minutes until nicely browned.

4 SERVINGS

Clam Fritters

These are wonderful for Sunday morning breakfast with corn bread.

2 cups clams, drained and chopped fine
4 eggs
1 cup milk
1 teaspoon baking powder
2 cups flour
1 teaspoon salt

Combine all ingredients and drop by spoonfuls into deep fat or fry in buttered skillet as for pancakes.

4 SERVINGS

It is highly possible that taverns marked as having poor fare were serving a one-dish supper variously called Shipwreck, Six Layer Dinner, and Hallejuh, although we found it an excellent family meal when accompanied by a salad and Buttermilk Biscuits (using the biscuit recipe for Onion Shortcake). Today we probably would not patronize a restaurant serving such homely food, although after a day on a stagecoach anything would be welcome.

Six Layer Dinner

2 cups potatoes, peeled and sliced thin
2 cups diced celery
1 cup chopped green pepper
1 pound ground lean beef
1 cup sliced onions
2 cups canned tomatoes, drained
Salt to taste
Freshly ground pepper

Preheat oven to 325°.
In a deep 3-quart casserole, layer ingredients in order given. Season each layer liberally.
Cover and bake for 2 hours.

4 SERVINGS

A letter from a young man who was a student at Yale in New Haven was amusing in that he was complaining about the food — salt pork, dried cod, and stewed oysters — and mentions that they were all tired of shelling their own peas for dinner! It shows that there is nothing new in student complaints about school food.

Quite a few recipes lay claim to Connecticut as their birthplace, such as Connecticut Bean Pot Stew and Connecticut Peach Pudding. The stew resembles any that we might make today, full of beef and seasonal vegetables, all simmered slowly in a bean pot. The Peach Pudding is interesting because we tend to forget that Connecticut is an orchard state; a farm diary from 1817 includes the following:

"Transplanted gooseberry bushes and pruned peach trees — 1 hand, 4 hrs."
"Set apple tree grafts."
"Went to Hartford to Horticultural exhibition and saw a number of varieties of the most celebrated apples, pears, peaches and plums."
"Prince of Wales favorite peach."

Even today in Connecticut there are some fairly sizable orchards that produce peaches rivaling the best from Georgia.

Connecticut Peach Pudding

3 tablespoons butter or margarine	3 teaspoons baking powder
⅓ cup brown sugar	½ cup milk
1 tablespoon fruit brandy	5 large ripe peaches
Grated rind of 1 lemon	1 tablespoon lemon juice
2 eggs, separated	½ cup sugar mixed with 1 teaspoon cinnamon
1 cup flour	
½ teaspoon salt	2 tablespoons sugar

Preheat oven to 350°.

Cream butter and brown sugar until smooth. Beat in brandy, lemon rind and 2 egg yolks.

Combine flour, salt, and baking powder. Add alternately to first mixture with milk. Beat well.

In shallow 2-quart baking dish, place skinned peach halves. Sprinkle with lemon juice and sugar mixed with cinnamon. Pour batter over all.

Bake for 25 to 30 minutes. Remove from oven.

Beat egg whites until stiff, gradually adding 2 tablespoons sugar. Spread over pudding. Bake for 10 minutes longer.

4 SERVINGS

My Scottish great-grandmother gave credence to the stories about the thrifty Scots. Her idea of ice cream was junket, pale, white, and watery. But the recipes she brought with her as a bride showed another side to the Scottish nature, one that loved sweets such as Hedgehog Pudding stuffed with raisins and almonds, shortbreads, rich cream scones, and Plum Cake.

Hedgehog Pudding

½ cup brandy
2 cups raisins
½ pound beef suet, chopped fine
1 cup sugar
1 teaspoon salt
1 teaspoon nutmeg
2 cups heavy cream
3 egg yolks
2 cups flour
1 cup bread crumbs
2 egg whites, beaten stiff
1 cup blanched almonds, slivered
4 tablespoons melted butter
2 tablespoons sugar

Heat brandy and pour over raisins in bowl. Soak for 1 hour. Drain raisins and put in bottom of 2-quart bowl or pudding mold.
Cream suet with 1 cup sugar. Add salt and nutmeg.
With fork, mix cream, egg yolks, and brandy drained from raisins.
Into suet mixture beat flour and crumbs alternately with cream mixture. Fold in beaten whites.
Pour into bowl over raisins. Cover securely with foil and tie.
Put bowl on rack in pan of simmering water that comes two thirds of the way up sides of bowl. Cover and steam for 3 hours.
Unmold onto serving platter. Stick slivered almonds all over pudding. Pour melted butter over all and sprinkle with 2 tablespoons sugar.

8 SERVINGS

Plum Cake

1 pound butter
2 cups sugar
2½ cups flour, sifted
8 eggs, separated
½ teaspoon mace

Grated rind of 1 lemon
½ teaspoon salt
2 tablespoons brandy
1 cup currants

Preheat oven to 300°.

Cream butter until very light. Gradually beat in sugar, again until very light. Beat in yolks one at a time alternately with ⅓ cup of flour. Blend in seasonings and brandy.

Beat whites until stiff and fold in.

Sprinkle flour over currants and fold gently into batter.

Pour into 2 greased 8 x 5-inch loaf pans, filling them two thirds full.

Bake for 1¼ to 1½ hours, until cakes test done. Turn out to cool on racks. Do not cut until completely cool. Best if left for at least a day.

YIELD: 2 LOAVES

Turning back to the sisters' diary for one more item of interest, I found an account of a prolonged visit to relatives who seemed to have an active social life, and certainly set a good table.

"We live extremely well and are in no danger of starving. Our dinners are excellent and buckwheat cakes plenty for breakfast with butter. In the evenings, friends come in and we have little suppers of biscuits and sweetmeats, nuts and fruits."

Buckwheat Cakes

½ package dry yeast
¼ cup lukewarm water
2 cups milk
1 cup buckwheat flour
1 cup white flour
½ teaspoon salt
2 tablespoons molasses
1 teaspoon baking soda
¼ cup warm water

Dissolve yeast in ¼ cup lukewarm water. Scald milk, then cool to lukewarm.

Beat together the yeast, milk, flours, salt, and molasses. Cover and let stand at room temperature overnight.

Next morning mix in the soda dissolved in ¼ cup warm water. Drop by spoonfuls onto hot greased griddle.

Serve with melted butter and maple syrup.

Rhode Island

Crab Cakes • 29
Scalloped Crab • 30
Panned Oysters • 30
Deep-dish Oyster Pie • 31
Fried Scallops • 32
Wakefield Kedgeree • 32
Molded Salmon with Cucumber Sauce • 34
Rhode Island Barrel Bake • 39
Jonnycake with Dried Beef Sauce • 40
Ham and Apple Pie • 35
Asparagus in Ambush • 36
A Mess O' Greens • 42
Newport Spice Cake • 36
Blackstone Pudding • 38
Peach Pan Dowdy • 38
Little Boy's Pudding • 39

APPARENTLY it was a copy of the Newport *Mercury* that prompted a visit by Agnes to some relatives in Rhode Island. An interesting, gossipy sheet, the paper started by James Franklin was full of news about the goings-on in this sophisticated, busy port. If one really wanted to see the highlights of New England life some hundred odd years ago, Newport was the place to be. The theater, discussion groups, musicales, "not one minute to spare from French music, balls and plays. This dissipation will be my undoing." Exactly what Agnes meant by this last we are not certain, but her frugal Scottish nature did not spurn the "seafood in every form, cakes of crab, escalloped crab, oysters panned and in pyes, scallops from the bay on our doorstep...."

Crab Cakes

1 pound crab meat	1 tablespoon dry mustard
1 egg	Salt to taste
¼ cup butter, melted	Freshly ground pepper
1 cup dry bread crumbs	Butter or oil for frying

Mix all ingredients together carefully. Shape into flat oval patties and refrigerate for an hour or more.

In large skillet heat butter to cover bottom of pan. Saute crab cakes until golden brown on each side. Or fry in deep fat until golden.

4 SERVINGS

Scalloped Crab

2 cups (1 pint) fresh-picked crab meat
2 tablespoons butter or margarine
2 tablespoons flour
1 cup rich milk or half and half
Salt to taste
½ teaspoon paprika
Freshly ground pepper
⅔ cup cracker crumbs
3 tablespoons melted butter

Preheat oven to 350°.
Heat butter in saucepan. Stir in flour and cook 2 minutes. Add milk and cook, stirring, until thick and smooth. Season to taste with salt, paprika, and pepper.
In shallow 1-quart baking dish layer ingredients: half of sauce, crab, remaining sauce, crumbs. Pour melted butter over top.
Bake for 20 minutes, until heated through.

4 SERVINGS

Panned Oysters

¼ cup butter
1 pint oysters, drained
Salt to taste
Freshly ground pepper
Dash of hot pepper sauce
¼ cup sherry
Hot buttered toast

Heat butter in skillet. Add oysters and cook over medium heat until edges curl. Season with salt and pepper.
Place toast slices on serving plates and cover with oysters. Keep warm.
Pour sherry into skillet, turn heat to high, and boil until liquid is slightly reduced, about 3 minutes.
Pour over oysters. Serve immediately.

4 SERVINGS

Deep-Dish Oyster Pie

4 tablespoons butter or margarine
2 tablespoons minced onion
½ cup diced celery
3 tablespoons flour
2 cups oysters, drained
   Oyster liquor plus milk to make
     2 cups liquid
Salt to taste
Freshly ground pepper
½ teaspoon mace
Pastry for top crust

In large saucepan heat butter. Add onion and celery and saute until soft, about 5 minutes.

Stir in flour and cook for 2 minutes. Add liquid and cook, stirring, until thickened and smooth. Add oysters and cook until edges curl. Season.

Pour mixture into greased 1-quart baking dish and cool.

Preheat oven to 400°.

Put on top crust and seal edges. Bake for 25 to 30 minutes, until crust is golden.

NOTE: This pie is also good made with half chicken and half oysters.

5 TO 6 SERVINGS

Fried Scallops

1 pint bay scallops (or sea scallops cut into smaller pieces)
¼ cup flour
Salt to taste
Freshly ground pepper
6 tablespoons butter
½ cup white wine
2 tablespoons minced parsley

Dry scallops on paper towel. Mix salt and pepper with flour. Dust scallops with the seasoned flour.

Heat butter in large skillet. Saute scallops in butter, stirring frequently, for 5 to 7 minutes. Remove to warm platter.

Pour wine into skillet and bring to boil, stirring up brown bits in bottom of pan. Pour over scallops. Sprinkle with parsley.

4 SERVINGS

"There is much talk here of a man's right to vote, and rule by the people, but it does not interfere with the daily business of trade in rum and slaves. Last evening a play at Kings Arms Tavern, The Provoked Husband. Amusing. Afterwards a supper of Wakefield Kedgeree."

Wakefield Kedgeree

Curry powder was found in some recipes for kedgeree, not in others. We found it to be a distinct asset, in moderate amounts. This is an excellent dish for lunch or supper with a green vegetable or salad. You might garnish it with chutney.

2 cups flaked cooked fish (haddock, finnan haddie, salmon)
2 cups hot cooked rice
½ cup cream
3 hard-boiled eggs, chopped
Salt to taste
Freshly ground pepper
1 tablespoon chopped parsley
1 teaspoon curry powder or to taste

Mix all ingredients together gently and place in double boiler. Heat over hot water and serve immediately.

NOTE: Can be heated in large, heavy saucepan over medium heat, stirring gently.

4 SERVINGS

In a letter to one of her children, Agnes describes the famous Trinity Church:

"A church built to look out to sea from whence come their fortunes. We attended to hear Bishop Berkeley but I was so taken with the three tier wine glass pulpit that it was hard to keep attention on his words. The whole interior lit by brass chandeliers with pyramids of tapers. We took dinner with friends in a home nearby and the Bishop with us so I talked to him not distracted by the surroundings. A pretty dish of salmon molded with sauce, pie made of the Rhode Island apple (greening), an elegant dish of new green asparagus in ambush and cake with spices from John's own cargo of last week. A walk around to see that very ship later."

Molded Salmon

1 pound cooked fresh or canned salmon
1 cup milk
1 cup bread crumbs
Salt to taste
Freshly ground pepper
½ teaspoon paprika
1 tablespoon lemon juice
3 eggs, separated

Preheat oven to 350°.
Pick over salmon and put into large bowl. Mash well.
Bring milk to scalding with bread crumbs in saucepan. Pour over salmon. Mix in salt, pepper, paprika, lemon juice, and egg yolks. Blend well.
Beat whites until stiff but not dry. Fold into salmon mixture. Put into well-greased loaf pan or ring mold.
Set pan in larger pan of hot water. Bake for 1 hour, until firm.
Remove mold from hot water. Let stand for 5 minutes. Run a knife around edge and unmold onto platter.
Serve hot with Cucumber sauce.

6 SERVINGS

Cucumber Sauce

1 cup sour cream
1 teaspoon sugar
1 tablespoon vinegar
1 cucumber, peeled, seeded, and chopped fine
1 tablespoon chopped dill or dried dill

Mix all ingredients together and chill until ready to serve.

Ham and Apple Pie

This is an inexpensive and filling supper dish and what is left over can be served for breakfast.

1 pound cooked ham, diced into ½-inch pieces
5 cups peeled, sliced tart apples
½ teaspoon pepper
¾ cup brown sugar
½ teaspoon cinnamon
½ teaspoon mace
½ teaspoon salt
1 recipe short pastry

Grease a deep 1½-quart baking dish. Put one-third of apples on bottom, half of ham on apples. Sprinkle with half of seasonings and sugar. Layer another third of the apples, remaining ham, and seasonings. Cover with remaining apples. Put on top crust of pastry and seal edges.

Preheat oven to 325°.

Bake for 1¾ hours. If crust becomes too brown, cover with foil.

Serve warm with cheese.

4 TO 5 SERVINGS

Asparagus in Ambush

This is a very pretty and unusual way of serving asparagus, much preferable to a soggy piece of toasted bread.

1 pound asparagus
4 French rolls (rectangular)
2 tablespoons butter
½ cup heavy cream, Bechamel sauce, or Hollandaise sauce.

Break off white part of asparagus stems. Trim stems up to heads with vegetable peeler.

Place asparagus stalks flat in large skillet. Cover with salted water halfway up stalks. Cover skillet. Place over high heat and bring to boil. Reduce heat and cook 5 to 7 minutes, until thickest part of stem is tender. Drain on paper towels.

Cut off tops of rolls and hollow out, making a case. Butter insides of rolls and tops.

Just before serving, heat rolls. Put stalks of asparagus inside (cut to fit) each roll, running the length of the roll. Pour cream, Bechamel sauce, or Hollandaise over each and put on cover.

Heat for 5 minutes at 350°. Serve immediately.

4 SERVINGS

Newport Spice Cake

1 egg
1 cup brown sugar
1 tablespoon molasses
1 cup flour
1 teaspoon cinnamon
1 teaspoon nutmeg
½ teaspoon cloves
1 teaspoon salt
1½ teaspoons baking soda
1 teaspoon cream of tartar
½ cup buttermilk
⅓ cup melted butter or margarine

Preheat oven to 375°.

In large bowl beat egg with sugar and molasses until thick.

Combine all dry ingredients. Add buttermilk and dry ingredients alternately to egg mixture, beating well. Stir in melted shortening.

Pour into greased 8-inch square tin. Bake for 25 to 30 minutes.

"Visited Martha's sister, Bertha, for a few days at her plantation at Narragansett. Her husband most proud of his saddle horse, a Narragansett Pacer. Many slaves do the work of farming. Our weather clear and dry. Good for growing. Benjamin's new orchards doing well. Jonathans good for Blackstone Pudding and we all enjoyed Peach Pan Dowdy with hard sauce, although little Timothy's favorite is his Little Boy's Pudding."

Blackstone Pudding

2 cups milk
3 tablespoons white corn meal
¼ cup dark molasses
½ teaspoon salt
½ teaspoon ginger
2 medium cooking apples

Put milk into top of double boiler. Bring to boiling point and stir in corn meal. Do not let lumps form. Put over boiling water and stir in molasses, salt, and ginger. Cover and cook for 30 minutes.

Preheat oven to 275°.

Pare and core apples and cut into eighths. Spread apples over bottom of greased 1½-quart baking dish. Pour corn meal mixture over apples.

Bake for 3 hours. Serve warm with hard sauce or ice cream.

4 TO 5 SERVINGS

Peach Pan Dowdy

3 cups sliced peaches
½ teaspoon nutmeg
½ teaspoon cinnamon
Juice of ½ lemon
⅓ cup brown sugar, packed
¼ cup butter or margarine
⅓ cup granulated sugar
1 egg
¾ cup flour
1 teaspoon baking powder
½ teaspoon salt
⅓ cup milk

Place peaches, nutmeg, cinnamon, lemon juice, and brown sugar in saucepan. Stew gently over medium heat until fruit is soft.

Preheat oven to 300°.

Place peach mixture in greased deep baking dish (1½-quart).

Cream butter and granulated sugar until light. Beat in egg. Beat in mixed dry ingredients together alternately with milk. Beat until smooth.

Spread over peaches. Bake for 30 minutes. Serve warm.

6 SERVINGS

Little Boy's Pudding

¾ cup rice
¾ cup sugar
6 tablespoons butter, melted
1 quart milk
½ teaspoon grated nutmeg
1 teaspoon cinnamon
½ teaspoon salt

Preheat oven to 275°.
Mix all ingredients together and and pour into 2-quart baking dish. Bake for 3 hours, stirring frequently during first hour.

8 SERVINGS

While at Narragansett, Agnes was treated to that wonderful production, a Rhode Island Barrel Bake, and she records it in detail. Here are the directions, put into modern terms by a master of the art, Stanley Ward, who has been doing these bakes for 50 years.

Rhode Island Barrel Bake
(Courtesy of Stanley Ward)

To prepare a bake for 8 hungry people:
To begin with, you need a barrel (mackerel, fish, or sugar).
In an open fire, heat rocks as hot as you can get them.
Meanwhile, pick over 1 bushel clams and discard any that are broken or opened. Wash clams thoroughly.
Put a layer of clean rockweed into barrel. Then put in hot stones and another layer of rockweed.
Tie clams, fish fillets, corn in the husk, unpeeled potatoes, sausages, and lobsters up in cloth or cheesecloth bags for easier removal.
Add in that order, putting into barrel quickly in order not to lose heat. Put a layer of rockweed over all; then tie canvas over the top.
Let cook for 1 to 1¼ hours.

A last note on this gay trip to Rhode Island:

"Finally, one evening at home with Martha and John to gossip about family and exchange receipts. Martha made up her receipt for Jonnycake. She says that the special corn meal is needed (fine ground and white) and we drove to the mill for it. Her cakes are thin with sauce of beef from their smokehouse. We had a salad of new greens with it. Will be sorry to leave this fine family."

Jonnycake

1 cup white stone-ground corn meal
1 teaspoon salt
1 cup boiling water
¼ cup milk

Put corn meal and salt into bowl. Add boiling water in a slow steady stream while stirring constantly. Mixture should not lump.

Stir in milk to make a thickish batter that plops, not drips, off spoon; about 3 tablespoons should be enough.

Heat an iron skillet or griddle. When a drop of water sizzles on it, brush with fat. Drop batter by spoonfuls; it is the right consistency if it starts to spread slowly when it hits the pan. Turn when browned. These take longer to cook than pancakes.

YIELD: 14 2-INCH CAKES

Dried Beef Sauce

½ pound old-fashioned smoked dried beef
6 tablespoons butter
5 tablespoons flour

¼ cup sour cream
1 cup milk
1 cup cream

Separate slices of beef and tear into smaller pieces.

Heat butter in large skillet and add beef. Saute for 2 minutes.

Stir in flour and cook for 2 minutes. Stir in sour cream, milk, and cream. Cook for 5 minutes. Serve hot over Jonnycakes.

YIELD: SUFFICIENT FOR
14 JONNYCAKES

A Mess O' Greens

1 pound mixed greens, including dandelion
4 slices bacon or lean salt pork
¼ cup sugar
¼ cup vinegar
1 teaspoon mustard
1 tablespoon chopped mint
Salt to taste
Freshly ground pepper

Wash and dry greens well and place in large salad bowl.

In skillet fry bacon until crisp. Drain and crumble.

To fat remaining in pan add sugar, vinegar, and mustard. Heat, stirring, until sugar is dissolved.

Pour over greens and toss with mint, salt, pepper, and bacon.

4 SERVINGS

Massachusetts

Fish Chowder • 62
Barley Vegetable Soup • 56
Spicy Salt Cod and Potatoes • 64
Salmon with Egg Sauce • 46
Baked Shad • 57
Shad Roe • 57
Braised Shoulder of Lamb • 55
Beef and Kidney Pie • 53
Baked Spareribs • 58
Baked Carrots and Potatoes • 52
Jerusalem Artichokes • 61
Brown Bread • 54
Portuguese Bread • 63
Shrewsbury Cakes • 47
Chocolate Puffs • 48
Gingerbread • 46
Indian Pudding Durgin Park • 48
Apple Toot • 50
Marlborough Pie • 50
Upside-down Apple Tart • 51
Deep-dish Cranberry Pie • 60
Molasses Taffy • 59

AGNES PETTIGREW'S uncle had settled in Massachusetts some years earlier and his children, her cousins, had scattered themselves about the New England states. The more adventurous had taken it upon themselves to go into the unsettled territories, becoming farmers or tradesmen, or shipbuilders in thriving coastal communities. Others stayed closer to home, settling in small Massachusetts towns; although one female cousin married and lived in the busy port of Boston. A visit to her town house was described in a letter:

> "The finest silk covers the walls and the table is set with polished silver and English crystal in great supply.
> "We went to the great market at Faneuil Hall this morning. It was much like London with prices the same. Fine fresh cod, smelts and salmon in great plenty. Saturday night we have oysters, then a boiled salmon with sauce of egg. The desserts include fresh fruits, pies, sage cheese and a light gingerbread that I especially like."

While the colonists were still sympathetic to the King, it was customary to support the fisheries by eating fish every Saturday night.

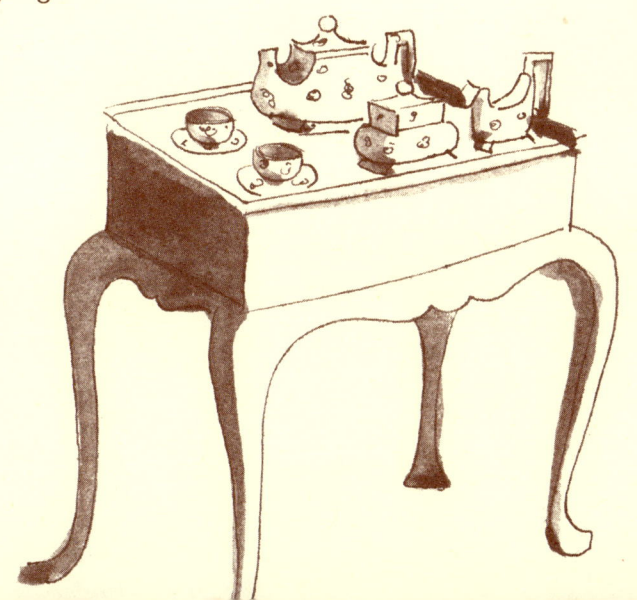

Salmon with Egg Sauce

3 to 4 pound salmon steak	1 teaspoon salt
Juice of 1 lemon	2 celery tops with leaves

Wrap salmon in cheesecloth, leaving long ends for "handles."

Half fill a fish poacher, steamer, or large roasting pan with water. Put in lemon juice, salt, and celery tops. Bring to a boil. Lower heat.

Put fish into water, leaving ends of cheesecloth out. Cover. Simmer (do not boil) fish for 8 minutes per pound.

Remove fish, unwrap, and place on warm platter.

6 TO 8 SERVINGS

Egg Sauce

2 tablespoons butter	Freshly ground pepper
2 tablespoons flour	¼ teaspoon paprika
1 cup rich milk or half and half	2 hard-boiled eggs, chopped fine
Salt to taste	

Melt butter in saucepan. Stir in flour and cook for 2 minutes. Add milk and cook, stirring until thick and smooth.

Season to taste. Stir in chopped eggs.

Pour over salmon.

6 TO 8 SERVINGS

Gingerbread

2 cups flour	½ cup molasses
2 tablespoons ginger	½ cup butter or margarine
1 teaspoon baking soda	½ cup water
½ teaspoon salt	1 egg

Preheat oven to 325°.
Put flour, ginger, baking soda, and salt in large bowl.
Combine molasses, butter, and water in saucepan. Bring to boil.
Boil until butter is melted. Stir into dry ingredients. Stir in egg.
Pour into greased 9 inch square pan. Bake for 25 minutes.
Serve with whipped cream and chocolate sauce.

Life was busy in Boston and my great-great-grandmother went to tea parties every afternoon, where a favorite spice cake called a Whig was served, along with Shrewsbury cakes, Naples biscuits (really ladyfingers), and chocolate puffs. The Baker Chocolate Company had its beginnings in 1765 on the banks of the Neponset River and chocolate was popular as a drink as well as a flavoring.

Shrewsbury Cakes

1 cup butter
½ cup powdered sugar
1 egg

1 tablespoon caraway seeds
2 cups flour
Raspberry jam

In mixing bowl beat together the butter and sugar. Add egg and mix well. Stir in caraway seeds. Mix in flour.
Preheat oven to 350°.
Roll dough out on board, ¼ inch thick. Cut in 2 inch circles.
Bake for 10 minutes. Serve hot with raspberry jam.

YIELD: 24 CAKES

Chocolate Puffs

4 egg whites
¾ cup sugar
4 tablespoons cocoa

Beat whites until foamy. Gradually beat in sugar and cocoa. Continue to beat until stiff and glossy.
Preheat oven to 300°.
Drop walnut-sized spoonfuls on lightly greased baking sheet. Bake for 30 to 40 minutes.

YIELD: 24 PUFFS

Agnes also mentions the custom of serving the pudding as a first course, followed by the meats and vegetables. What appetites they must have had to go through a large serving of Indian Pudding before starting on the main part of the meal.

Indian Pudding Durgin Park

There are numerous recipes for this famous New England dish, but after trying six different ones I settled on this version as being the closest to the Indian Pudding I remember eating as a child. The two most important details are long slow cooking and dark molasses.

1 cup yellow stone-ground corn meal
½ cup black molasses
¼ cup sugar
¼ cup lard or butter
¼ teaspoon salt
¼ teaspoon baking soda
2 eggs
1½ quarts hot milk

Preheat oven to 450°.

Mix all ingredients thoroughly with one half of the hot milk. Pour into a well-greased non-metal baking dish. Bake until mixture boils.

Turn oven to 300°. Stir in remaining hot milk and bake for 5 to 7 hours.

Serve warm with cream or vanilla ice cream.

10 TO 12 SERVINGS
RECIPE CAN BE HALVED.

Agnes' Uncle Charles was really a farmer, well to do for the times (late eighteenth century) but living a simpler life than some of the Boston relatives. Agnes visited him out of duty, I have a feeling, because she seemed to find life in the country a bit dull compared to life with the city cousins. Farm food was plentiful and nourishing but simpler and more repetitious in content.

> *"Uncle Charles is prideful of his orchards, especially the apples with every variety and many I don't know at all. We eat them at every meal in some form. A dessert for the children called Apple Toot had raisins as well. The Marlborough Pie used Roxbury Russets and another pie with Gravensteins was turned over at the finish to put the crust on the bottom."*

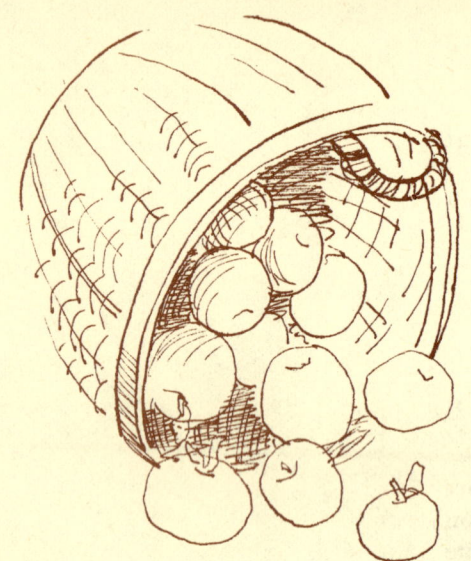

Apple Toot

2 eggs
½ cup maple syrup
1½ tablespoons flour
2 teaspoons baking powder
½ teaspoon salt
1 large apple, peeled and diced
¼ cup dried currants
¼ cup raisins

Preheat oven to 350°.
Put eggs in large bowl. Beat in maple syrup. Beat in flour, baking powder, and salt, sifted together. Stir in apple, raisins, and currants.
Pour into buttered 1½-quart baking dish. Bake for 35 to 40 minutes, until puffed and golden. Serve with a custard sauce.

4 TO 5 SERVINGS

Marlborough Pie

½ cup plain thick applesauce
½ cup sugar
⅔ cup coffee cream
Grated rind and juice of 1 lemon
1 teaspoon nutmeg
3 eggs
Unbaked 9-inch pastry shell

Preheat oven to 425°.

In large bowl combine applesauce with sugar, cream, lemon juice, lemon rind, and nutmeg. Beat in eggs one at a time, blending well. Pour into pastry shell.

Bake for 10 minutes. Reduce heat to 325° and bake 35 to 40 minutes, until set. Let cool before cutting.

6 SERVINGS

Upside-Down Apple Tart

The upside-down tart sounds like a French version of the same thing with the elegant name of Tarte Tatin. It should be turned out onto a plate that indents slightly to allow for the curve in the top crust.

5 large tart apples, pared and thinly sliced	2 tablespoons flour
	½ teaspoon nutmeg
3 tablespoons butter	1 teaspoon cinnamon
2 tablespoons maple syrup	Pastry for top crust
⅔ cup brown sugar	

Preheat oven to 450°

Spread a 9-inch pie pan with 1 tablespoon butter and the maple syrup.

In large bowl toss apple slices with sugar, flour, and spices. Fill pie pan with apples. Dot with remaining butter.

Cover with pastry crust, crimping to edges of pan. Slit pastry in four spots with knife.

Bake for 10 minutes. Turn heat to 350° and bake for 30 minutes. Cool slightly.

Loosen pastry crust from pan with point of sharp knife. Invert onto rounded plate.

Serve warm with whipped cream.

6 SERVINGS

"Cider is plentiful and even the children drink it for breakfast, dinner and supper. Vegetables are good and fresh. Aunt Hat bakes carrots and potatoes together. These for dinner with beef and kidney pie. Cold meat and good brown bread for supper."

Baked Carrots and Potatoes

4 carrots	Freshly ground pepper
3 large potatoes	¼ teaspoon ginger
Salt to taste	1 cup cream

Peel carrots and cut into matchstick pieces. Peel potatoes and cut the same size and shape as carrots.

Preheat oven to 350°.

Butter a 1½-quart baking dish. Arrange half of carrot sticks in bottom. Put half of potato sticks crosswise over carrots. Sprinkle with salt, pepper, and ginger. Repeat vegetables. Pour in cream.

Cover and bake for 1 hour, until liquid is absorbed and vegetables are tender.

4 TO 5 SERVINGS

Beef and Kidney Pie

2 pounds lean beef, cut in 1-inch cubes
¼ pound kidney, cut in small pieces
1 tablespoon flour
¼ teaspoon mace
1 teaspoon salt
Freshly ground pepper
2 tablespoons butter
1 tablespoon oil
1 cup beef bouillon
¾ cup port wine
1 bay leaf
1 tablespoon Worcestershire sauce
½ pound mushrooms
2 hard boiled eggs
Pastry for top crust

Preheat oven to 300°.

Dredge beef cubes and kidney pieces in flour seasoned with mace, salt, and pepper.

Heat oil and butter to bubbling in large skillet. Brown meats on all sides. Do not crowd pan. As they are browned, remove to 1½-quart casserole.

Add any flour left from dredging to skillet. Cook briefly. Pour in bouillon and bring to a boil. Pour over meat.

Add remaining ingredients except eggs to casserole. Cover and bake for 2 to 3 hours, until meat is very tender. Remove from oven and cool (Could be simmered on top of stove instead of baked.)

Preheat oven to 400°.

Put sliced hard-boiled eggs over top of meat. Cover with pastry crust. Bake for 30 minutes, until crust is browned. Serve immediately.

6 SERVINGS

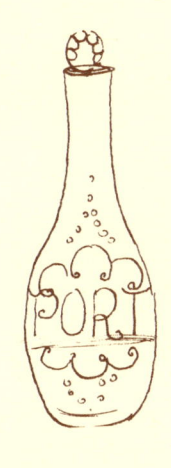

Brown Bread

This bread freezes well and is even better the second day.

1 cup yellow corn meal	2 teaspoons baking soda
1 cup white flour	¼ cup maple syrup
1 cup whole wheat or graham flour	½ cup molasses
1 teaspoon salt	2 cups buttermilk

Put all dry ingredients in large bowl. Add maple syrup, molasses, and buttermilk. Mix together thoroughly.

Fill two well-greased 1-quart molds, coffee cans, or bowls half full. Cover tightly.

Place on rack in large pan of simmering water. Cover pan and steam for 3 hours.

When done, remove covers and place in 350° oven for 5 minutes to dry out.

To reheat, wrap bread in foil and place in 350° oven.

A letter from one of the family who lived in the Connecticut Valley talks of "my herbes that will be ready soon for picking and drying. I planted more this season, with much savory for our soups, dill for the mutton stews and lamb shoulder."

Lamb shoulder is interesting to us because we are much more inclined toward the leg, but the early housewives knew how to bone and braise the shoulder, or flatten and broil it.

Braised Shoulder of Lamb

1 shoulder of lamb, 4 to 4½ pounds, boned and tied, with most of fat removed
2 tablespoons oil
Salt to taste
Freshly ground pepper
3 whole cloves garlic
2 medium onions, peeled and chopped
1 rutabaga, peeled and diced
2 carrots, peeled and quartered
4 sprigs fresh dill or 2 teaspoons dried dill
½ cup water
1 tablespoon chopped dill
1 tablespoon chopped parsley

Heat oil in deep heavy pan and brown lamb on all sides. Pour off fat.

Add salt, pepper, garlic cloves, onions, rutabaga, and carrots to lamb. Pour in water and place dill sprigs on top of meat.

Cover and simmer over low heat for 1½ to 2 hours, until meat is tender but not dry. Transfer meat to warm platter and remove strings. Sprinkle with chopped dill and parsley.

6 TO 8 SERVINGS

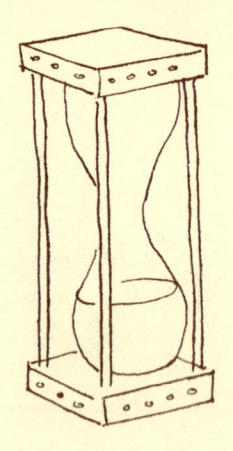

Barley Vegetable Soup

2 tablespoons butter
1 medium onion, chopped
2 stalks celery, diced
2 carrots, peeled and diced
1 meaty soup bone
1 cup peeled and chopped tomatoes
2 medium potatoes, peeled and diced
1 yellow turnip, peeled and diced
1 quart of water
Salt to taste
Freshly ground pepper
1 teaspoon savory
½ teaspoon thyme
½ cup barley
½ cup each lima beans, corn, and peas
2 tablespoons chopped parsley

In large soup kettle heat butter. Saute onion, celery, and carrots until glazed — about 5 minutes. Add soup bone, tomatoes, potatoes, turnip, and water. Season to taste and add herbs.

Cover and simmer for 2 to 3 hours, until broth is well flavored. Add barley and remaining vegetables and simmer until done.

Check seasoning and garnish with parsley.

4 TO 6 SERVINGS

This same young lady also mentions the abundance of shad, which at that time crowded the rivers in the spring and was considered a very ordinary fish. How I envy her; although the shad is starting to come back in greater supply, we still consider it a treat.

Baked Shad

6 tablespoons butter
2 sides of boned shad (about 2 pounds)
Salt to taste
Freshly ground pepper
¼ cup dry white wine

Preheat oven to 350°.
Put butter in shallow baking dish that will hold fish in one layer. Put dish in oven until butter melts.
Coat fish on both sides with butter. Lay flat and season lightly with salt and pepper. Pour wine over fish.
Bake for 45 minutes, basting occasionally.
To test fish for doneness, put fork into thickest part of flesh. If tines pull out easily and fish flakes, it is ready to serve.

6 SERVINGS

Shad Roe

1 pair shad roe
½ tablespoon salt
1 tablespoon vinegar
3 tablespoons butter
Juice of ½ lemon
1 tablespoon minced parsley

Prick with needle in several places and place roe in skillet and cover with boiling water. Add salt and vinegar.
Cover and simmer over low heat for 5 to 15 minutes, depending on size of roe, until roe is white. Drain.
Cover with cold water and let stand 5 minutes. Drain and dry.
Heat butter in skillet and saute roe for about 10 minutes. Roe should be firm but not dry or hard.
Remove roe to heated platter and add lemon juice to pan with 1 tablespoon butter. Bring to boil and swirl pan until butter is melted.
Pour over roe and garnish with parsley.

2 SERVINGS

Excerpt from a diary dated 1802 written by a lady named Hannah. How she fitted into the family I do not know, but she sounds gay and interesting.

"J. and I attended Mrs. Buton's funeral. Sad day. We dined well on roast partridge, ribs and sweet puddings.
"Invitation arrived in today's post to a sleighing party. Must think of my dress. A taffy pull afterward. Ate too many of Aunt Mag's good doughnuts. Dear Father brought me some books from town. "Gulliver's Travels" and "Myserties of Udolpho."

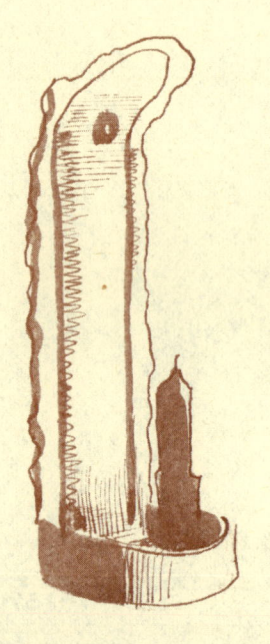

Baked Spareribs

3 pounds spareribs, cut into serving pieces	½ cup tomato puree or thick tomato sauce
1 cup boiling water	Salt to taste
½ cup maple syrup	Freshly ground pepper
½ cup cider	1 onion, chopped

Preheat oven to 450°.
Place ribs on rack over baking pan and bake in hot oven for 15 minutes. Remove from oven and turn heat down to 350°. Pour boiling water into pan under ribs.
Heat together the maple syrup, cider, and tomato puree or sauce.
Season the ribs. Spread with onion and one third of syrup mixture. Bake for 1½ hours, basting until all mixture is used up.

4 SERVINGS

I introduced my children to an old-fashioned taffy pull on a rainy afternoon and thought, "Hurrah for the simple things in life." It was entirely new to them and a great success.

Molasses Taffy

1 cup granulated sugar
¾ cup brown sugar
2 cups molasses
1 cup water
¼ cup butter or margarine
1/8 teaspoon baking soda
¼ teaspoon salt

In large heavy saucepan put sugars, molasses, and water. Boil together until thermometer registers 270°.

Remove from heat and add butter, baking soda, and salt. Mix well. Grease a large baking pan and pour in mixture. Cool. In about 10 minutes it will be cool enough to be pulled.

Butter fingers and work with taffy, pulling and twisting, until firm and pale in color. When ready, twist into a rope and cut into 2-inch lengths.

YIELD: ABOUT 48 PIECES

From inland to the coast was a long journey, even seventy-five years ago. In the late eighteenth or early nineteenth century it was hard traveling. But Agnes Pettigrew was a hardy Scot (she lived to be ninety-two) and it was her intention to see as much as she could in a lifetime. Besides, the Cape Cod region was so very different from the rest of New England that it was a challenge to her pioneer spirit. Her nieces and nephews who lived in the New Bedford area were much involved with ships and their lives were governed by the temperament of the sea. She comments on her visit:

"Bogs of cranberries as far as the eye can see and many dishes made of this slightly bitter berry which turns the land crimson at harvest time. Jellies and conserves, muffins and breads, pies and puddings till it seems we've had enough of the cranberry."

Deep-Dish Cranberry Pie

4 cups cranberries, chopped
1½ cups brown sugar
1½ tablespoons flour
2 tablespoons water
½ cup walnuts
2 tablespoons butter
2 tablespoons granulated sugar
Rich pastry for top crust

Preheat oven to 450°.
In large bowl mix cranberries with brown sugar, flour, water, and walnuts. Put mixture into deep 1-quart baking dish. Dot with butter. Cover with pastry. Sprinkle 2 tablespoons sugar over pastry.

Bake for 10 minutes. Turn heat down to 350° and bake for 30 minutes.

Serve warm with ice cream

6 SERVINGS

"The Jerusalem artichoke grows well here in the sandy soil and makes a nice change from the potato. It was said to be Indian food but I find it quite pleasant."

The Jerusalem artichoke is native to America and, being low in starch and sugar, is a valuable substitute for potatoes. It is a rough-looking tuber that must be scrubbed and peeled. Then it can be boiled until tender — 10 to 15 minutes, depending on the size — and served with butter, salt, and pepper.

"We have many chowders for breakfast and supper. They are made of fish, of which there is a plentiful supply. Sometimes

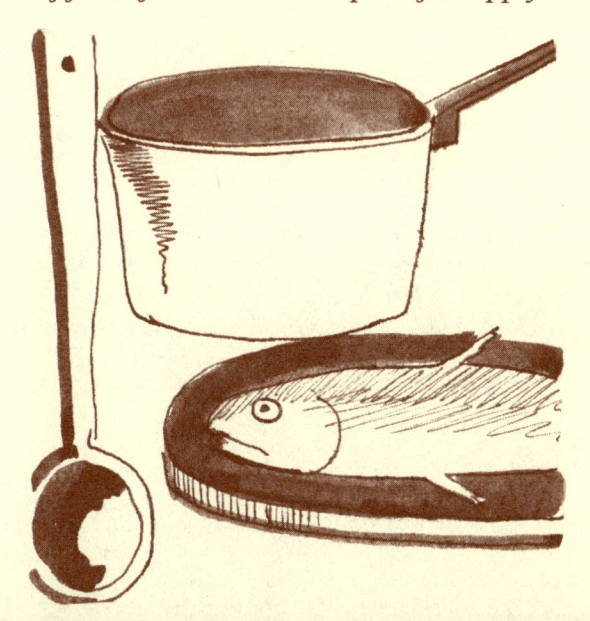

chicken or meat. It is said they are better the second day than the first and the third day better than the second."

Fish Chowder

¼ pound salt pork, diced
4 medium onions, peeled and sliced thin
4 medium potatoes, pared and diced

2 pounds haddock, cod or bass cut in 2-inch pieces
1 quart rich milk
Salt to taste
Freshly ground pepper

In large kettle heat salt pork and fry until crisp. Remove pork bits to paper towel.
In remaining fat saute onions until soft. Add potatoes and enough water to cover. Cook for 10 minutes.
Add fish, milk, and salt and pepper. Cover and simmer over lowest heat for 2 hours. Do not stir.
Serve in heated bowls with a pat of butter on each and pork bits sprinkled on top.

4 TO 6 SERVINGS

"New Bedford lives with the sea. The whaling schooners come and go and the women wait for their men to return. They are a brave lot and lonely much of the time as they must do work for both. Many Portuguese in this town. I find their diet not to my taste, all but the bread. I prefer my own receipt for salt cod, though admitting the other has a bit more spice."

Portuguese Bread

1 cup boiling water
3 teaspoons salt
6 tablespoons vegetable shortening
1 cup lukewarm water
1 package dry yeast
1 tablespoon sugar
6 cups flour

In large bowl put boiling water, salt, and shortening. Cool to lukewarm.

In lukewarm water combine yeast and sugar. Let stand until bubbly.

Stir yeast into first mixture. Add 4 cups flour and beat until smooth. Beat in remaining flour, mixing well.

Turn out onto floured board and knead until dough is smooth and elastic. Put dough in large greased bowl. Cover and let rise in warm spot until doubled in bulk, about 1 hour.

Punch down dough and divide in half. Shape each half into a round loaf 8 to 9 inches in diameter. Place in greased round tins (cake tins will do). Cover and let rise until again doubled in bulk.

Preheat oven to 400°.

Slash tops of loaves three times with sharp knife. Bake for 45 to 50 minutes, until done.

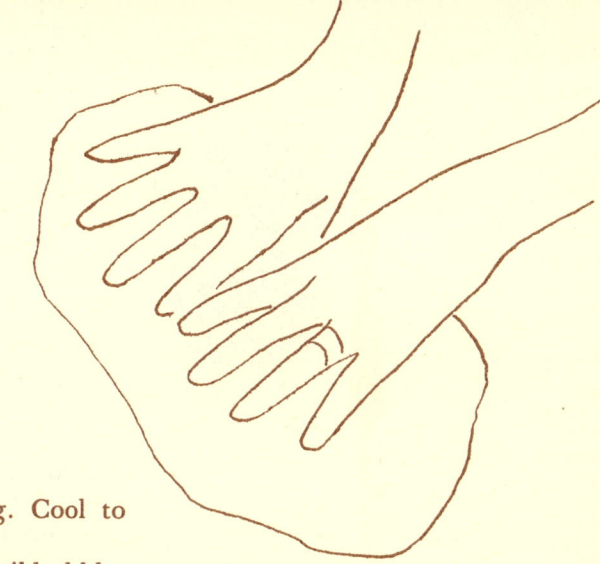

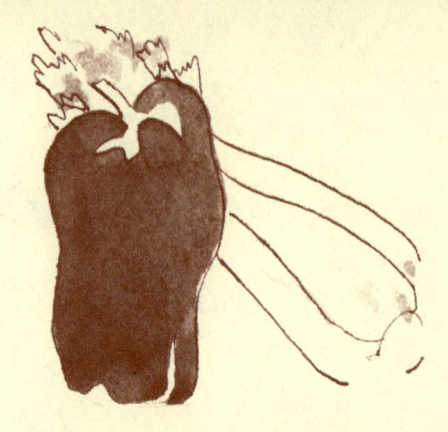

Spicy Salt Cod and Potatoes

1 pound salt cod
⅓ cup oil
3 onions, sliced thin
2 cloves garlic, minced
1 small green pepper, diced
2 stalks celery, diced
3 potatoes, peeled and sliced
½ teaspoon thyme
1 bay leaf
¼ teaspoon hot pepper flakes
1 cup chopped tomatoes
Freshly ground pepper
½ cup dry white wine
¼ cup bread crumbs
¼ cup grated Parmesan cheese

Soak codfish overnight in cold water. Drain, rinse, and drain again. Cut into 4-inch pieces.

In heavy kettle heat oil. Saute onions, garlic, green pepper, and celery until soft. Put in sliced potatoes. Cover with thyme, bay leaf, hot pepper flakes, and tomatoes. Put fish pieces on top of this mixture. Pour wine over all. Sprinkle with ground pepper.

Cover and simmer for 15 minutes, until potatoes are tender.

Dish can be prepared ahead to this point. When ready to serve, preheat oven to 325°.

Mix together the bread crumbs and cheese and sprinkle over top. Bake for 10 to 15 minutes, until heated through.

Serve with Portuguese Bread and a fruit dessert.

6 SERVINGS

New Hampshire

Cabbage Soup • 67
Cream of Green Pea Soup • 80
Grilled Trout • 75
Veal and Ham Pie • 72
Beef Olives • 81
Baked Stuffed Cucumbers • 72
Fried Potato Cakes • 76
Corn Pudding • 76
Lima Bean Pudding • 77
Planked Eggplant • 82
Oat Rolls • 68
Bannock • 70
Oatmeal Scones • 70
Soda Biscuits • 78
Washington Pie • 69
Molasses Sponge • 73
Black Walnut Cake • 74
Dorset Apple Cake • 79
Shoofly Pie • 82

THERE has always been rivalry among the colleges of New England, especially on the playing fields, but while the students at Yale were complaining about their stewed cod and oysters, it would seem that the young men at Dartmouth College in Hanover had a more legitimate complaint. A Dr. Belknap of Dover writes: "The scholars say they scarce ever have fresh meat and the victuals are very badly dressed." Even as late as 1881 a letter from a student states, "In the morning we have cold water and bread and butter only; meat at noon with two kinds of sauce and bread and cold water . . . . We have no tea, coffee, cider, milk; no meat but once a day, pyes only on Sunday."

Since the son of a Portsmouth relative was attending Eleazar Wheelock's college in the wilds of New Hampshire, Agnes decided to go as far as Portsmouth and find out what life was like in the northern part of New England. She traveled by stage from Boston to Portsmouth on the "Portsmouth Flyer," making a stop at the Earl of Halifax Inn where "the fare was plenty and reasonable with filling cabbage soup, oat rolls and Washington Pie."

Cabbage Soup

1 pound shoulder of lamb, well trimmed and cut into 1-inch cubes
1 tablespoon butter or margarine
1 tablespoon oil
1 onion, chopped
 Salt to taste
Freshly ground pepper
2 tablespoons chopped fresh dill weed
2 quarts water
1 large potato, peeled and diced
1 medium cabbage, shredded
1 tablespoon chopped parsley

Heat butter and oil in skillet. Brown lamb on all sides.
Add onion and saute until soft.
Put lamb, onion, salt, pepper, dill, and water into large kettle. Cover and bring to a boil.

Reduce heat and simmer for 1 hour, until meat is tender.
Add potato and cabbage. Cook another 30 minutes.
Serve with chopped parsley sprinkled on top.

6 SERVINGS

Oat Rolls

1 cup boiling water
½ cup regular oats
¼ cup butter, lard, or vegetable shortening
¼ cup molasses
2 teaspoons salt

1 package dry yeast
⅓ cup lukewarm water
1 egg
2 cups graham flour
1 cup white flour
Melted butter

In large bowl put boiling water, oats, shortening, molasses, and salt. Cool to lukewarm.

Dissolve yeast in ⅓ cup lukewarm water. Add to oat mixture.

Beat in egg.

Beat in graham flour and half of white flour.

Mix well, adding more flour if needed to make a soft but not sticky dough. It will be softer than bread dough.

Place in greased bowl, cover, and refrigerate for 2 to 3 hours.

Turn out, knead briefly, and shape into rolls.

Place in greased 2-inch muffin tins. Rolls should come halfway up sides.

Cover and let rise in warm place until double, 1½ to 2 hours.

Preheat oven to 375.°

Brush tops with melted butter and bake for 15 minutes.

YIELD: 18 ROLLS

Washington Pie

4 tablespoons butter or margarine
¾ cup sugar
1 egg
1½ cups flour
2 teaspoons baking powder
½ teaspoon salt
½ cup milk
1 teaspoon vanilla
Raspberry jam
Confectioners' sugar

Grease 2 8-inch layer cake pans.
Preheat oven to 350°.
In mixing bowl, beat butter and add sugar gradually, until light. Beat in egg.
Combine dry ingredients and mix in alternately with milk. Add vanilla and blend well.
Pour into layer cake tins. Bake for 25 minutes until done.
Turn out onto racks and cool.
Fill with raspberry jam between layers and sprinkle powdered confectioners' sugar on top.

Agnes felt quite at home in New Hampshire because of the Scottish and Irish settlements and their influence on the local foods with bannock and oatmeal scones high on the list of "plain" foods.

Bannock

This resembles Southern spoon bread and can be served for breakfast with maple syrup or as an accompaniment to ham or pork at dinner (with lots of butter).

2 cups milk
¾ cup yellow corn meal
1 teaspoon salt
1 tablespoon butter
3 eggs, separated

Scald milk in top of double boiler, slowly adding corn meal and stirring constantly.
Stir in salt and butter.
Cook over hot water until thick. Cool.
Preheat oven to 400°.
Beat in the egg yolks. Fold in stiffly beaten whites.
Pour into well-buttered 1½-quart baking dish and bake for 30 minutes, until set.

6 SERVINGS

Oatmeal Scones

1 cup flour
¼ cup regular oats
1 teaspoon cream of tartar
1 teaspoon baking soda
½ cup butter or half lard and half butter
1 egg beaten with ¼ cup cold water
½ teaspoon salt

Preheat oven to 450°.
In large bowl mix together dry ingredients.
Cut in shortening with pastry blender or fingertips until mixture resembles coarse meal.

Add egg and water and mix together quickly to form dough.

Roll out on floured board. Cut into diamond shapes or 3-inch circles.

Bake on lightly greased baking sheet for 12 to 15 minutes.

Split and eat hot with butter and jam.

YIELD: 8 SCONES

The bustling town of Portsmouth was another story. Here the Harvard-educated merchants and shipbuilders lived well.

"Much use of my lavender silk and lace gown," Agnes writes her daughter. "We dress for theater and dance assemblies, with late suppers of veal pies and turkey, baked cucumbers, molasses sponge and black walnut cakes."

Veal and Ham Pie

1 pound boneless veal cut into 1-inch cubes	¼ cup chicken broth
	2 cups cooked ham, cubed
1 leek, white part only sliced thin	2 hard-boiled eggs, chopped fine
1 shallot, chopped	⅓ cup cream
Salt to taste	2 tablespoons Madeire
Freshly ground pepper	Short pastry for top crust

Preheat oven to 325°.

Into heavy Dutch oven or baking dish put veal, leek, shallot, salt and pepper, and chicken broth. Cover and cook in oven for 1 hour.

Remove from oven and mix in ham, chopped eggs, and cream. Cool.

Pour veal and ham mixture into a shallow 1-quart baking dish.

Fit pastry over top, sealing edges. Poke a small hole in top.

Chill for one hour.

Preheat oven to 425°.

Bake pie for 40 minutes.

Pour Madeira through hole in top. Bake 5 minutes longer.

4 TO 5 SERVINGS

Baked Stuffed Cucumbers

2 large cucumbers	2 tablespoons grated onion
1 cup fine bread crumbs	½ cup bouillon
¼ cup grated Parmesan cheese	
1 tablespoon minced parsley or dill	

Peel cucumbers and cut in half across and a half lengthwise. Seed. Simmer in salted water until just tender. Cool.

Preheat oven to 350°.

Mix together the bread crumbs, cheese, herb, and onion. Fill cucumbers with this mixture.

Place in baking dish and pour bouillon around them.

Bake for 20 minutes.

6 to 8 servings

Molasses Sponge

4 eggs, separated	½ teaspoon cinnamon
¼ cup sugar	¼ teaspoon ginger
½ cup molasses	¼ teaspoon cloves
¼ teaspoon salt	½ teaspoon nutmeg

Preheat oven to 375°.

Beat egg whites, adding sugar gradually, until stiff.

In another bowl beat yolks with molasses, salt, and spices until thick.

Stir and cook yolk mixture over hot water until the spoon is coated.

Fold in whites.

Pour into greased 1½-quart baking dish. Bake about 15 minutes until lightly browned.

4 to 6 servings

Black Walnut Cake

½ cup butter or margarine
½ cup brown sugar
½ cup white sugar
3 egg whites
½ cup milk
1 ½ cups flour

1 ½ teaspoons baking soda
1 teaspoon cream of tartar
1 teaspoon milk
¾ cup black walnuts (or walnuts), coarsely chopped
Powdered sugar

Preheat oven to 350°.
In mixing bowl cream butter and sugar until light and smooth.
Beat egg whites until stiff and beat into butter mixture.
Beat in flour and milk alternately.
Dissolve soda and cream of tartar in 1 teaspoon milk. Stir into batter. Mix in walnuts.
Pour into buttered and floured 8 x 5-inch loaf pan.
Bake for 30 minutes, until cake is done.
When cool, sprinkle with powdered sugar.

New Hampshire was largely a rural society and outside of Portsmouth the people lived off the land, eating well and heartily. Agnes was determined to see Dartmouth college and on her way to Hanover she visited friends who lived a very rural life.

"Sarah sets a good table. Bean porridge for breakfast. Toasted bread, smoked dried beef, cheese and fish always from the lake. Our dinner set for the hands with potatoes fried in some fashion, game pies, much rabbit, puddings of dried beans or hulled corn. Soda biscuits for the children to spread with honey. Jab keeps ten hives."

Grilled Trout

3 trout, about 10 ounces each, cleaned, with gills removed
½ cup corn meal
Salt to taste
Freshly ground pepper
½ cup butter or bacon fat

Mix corn meal with salt and pepper. Dredge fish on both sides in meal.
Heat butter in large skillet or griddle to smoking. Lower heat to medium and cook trout for 5 to 7 minutes on one side. Turn fish and cook for 5 to 7 minutes on other side.
Test for doneness by inserting tines of fork into thickest part of fish. If fork pulls out easily fish is done.

3 OR 4 SERVINGS

Fried Potato Cakes

4 medium potatoes
½ cup flour
2 egg yolks beaten with
   1 tablespoon water
½ cup bread crumbs
4 tablespoons butter or margarine

Boil potatoes until tender but not mushy.
Cool, peel, and slice into ½-inch thick slices.
Dip potato slices into flour, egg yolk, and crumbs in that order.
Heat butter in large skillet. Saute potato slices until crisp and brown.

4 TO 6 SERVINGS

Corn Pudding

1 cup hulled corn, cooked (or 1 cup frozen corn kernels)
1 egg
1 cup rich milk
Salt to taste
Freshly ground pepper
1 teaspoon sugar
1 tablespoon melted butter or margarine

Preheat oven to 325°.
Mix all ingredients together in bowl. Pour into greased 1-quart baking dish.
Bake until firm, about 45 to 50 minutes.

6 SERVINGS

Lima Bean Pudding

3 cups dried lima beans
2 tablespoons butter
1 tablespoon oil
½ green pepper, chopped
1 small onion, chopped
3 stalks celery, chopped

Salt to taste
Freshly ground pepper
1 teaspoon dry mustard
1 cup tomato sauce
6 slices bacon

    Soak lima beans overnight in water to cover.
    Drain and put in large pot. Cover with water and bring to boil. Reduce heat to simmer, cover, and cook until tender. The time varies, so start checking beans after 30 minutes. Don't overcook.
    Drain and put into deep baking dish.
    Preheat oven to 350°.
    In skillet heat butter and oil. Saute green pepper, onion, and celery until soft.
    Stir in salt, pepper, mustard, and tomato sauce. Stir this mixture into beans. Put bacon slices over top.
    Bake for 30 minutes.

6 SERVINGS

Soda Biscuits
(From The Yankee Cookbook by Imogene Wolcott)

My children preferred these to baking powder biscuits, saying they are lighter and less crumbly. They warm over well.

2 cups flour	½ teaspoon salt
½ teaspoon soda	¼ cup lard
1 teaspoon cream of tartar	¾ cup milk

Preheat oven to 450°.
Put dry ingredients in large bowl. Cut in shortening.
Add milk until soft dough is formed.
Mix well and turn out onto floured board. Knead briefly. Pat to ½-inch thickness. Cut into 1½-2-inch biscuits.
Bake on ungreased baking sheet for 12 to 15 minutes.

YIELD: 18 TO 24 BISCUITS

"Yesterday a barn raising and I met many friends and neighbors. Cider in great barrels. Dorset Apple Cake to eat with doughnuts. Much game here. Sarah winters it over by filling hollows of dressed birds with snow and packing in barrels of snow."

Frozen foods are not new to New England, just the methods of preparation. We do know that colonial America's winters were colder than ours and it was easy to freeze foods solid by just keeping them outside.

Dorset Apple Cake

2 cups flour
1 cup shortening
½ teaspoon salt
3 teaspoons baking powder
1 pound tart apples (4 medium apples), pared and chopped fine
1 cup sugar
1 teaspoon cinnamon
½ teaspoon mace
¾ to 1 cup buttermilk

Preheat oven to 375°.

In large mixing bowl combine flour and shortening and work together until the consistency of coarse meal.

Stir in salt and baking powder.

In separate bowl mix together the apples, sugar, cinnamon, and mace.

Combine the two mixtures. Add ¾ cup of buttermilk to make a firm dough. Mix well.

Pat or roll into a flat cake about ¾-inch thick.

Place on baking sheet and bake for 45 to 55 minutes.

Serve hot with butter.

Agnes didn't make it to Hanover. It may have been the rough trip that deterred her or, more likely, an exciting invitation.

"Samuel and Abby asked to dine at Governor Wentworth's mansion and I may accompany them. Have heard much about his splendid estate. 6000 acres with stables and coachhouses. The main house very large and grand. A bad road from P. so we shall stop on the way."

Her account of the visit is detailed and the dinner menu impressive, especially the "soup of freshest green peas, beef olives, planked eggplant, blanc manage and a shoofly pie of rich sweetness."

Cream of Green Pea Soup

2 cups shelled fresh peas
A few pea pods
½ medium onion, finely chopped
6 cups chicken bouillon
1 large sprig fresh mint
Salt to taste
1 teaspoon sugar
1 cup cream
2 egg yolks

In large saucepan put peas, pods, onion, bouillon, mint, salt, and sugar. Put pot over high heat and bring to a boil. Lower heat, cover, and cook for 30 minutes.

Remove pods and puree soup in blender. Return to saucepan.

Before serving, stir in yolks blended with cream. Cook, stirring, for 5 minutes. Do not boil.

6 SERVINGS

Beef Olives

2 pounds beef round in one piece cut ¼-inch thick
3 tablespoons butter or margarine
2 tablespoons oil
1 medium onion, minced
1 clove garlic, minced
½ pound ham or veal, finely chopped
2 tablespoons chopped parsley
½ teaspoon thyme
2 tablespoons bread crumbs
1 egg (optional)
Salt to taste
Freshly ground pepper
Flour for dredging
1 cup beef bouillon
½ cup red wine
1 tablespoon flour mixed with 1 tablespoon butter
2 tablespoons chopped parsley

Cut beef into 12 equal pieces and pound until about 1/8-inch thick.

Heat 1 tablespoon butter and 1 tablespoon oil in skillet and saute onion and garlic until soft.

Stir in ham or veal, 2 tablespoons parsley, thyme, and bread crumbs. If too dry, add egg. Season with salt and pepper.

Spread mixture on beef slices. Roll up, tucking in ends, and tie with strings or thread. Dredge in flour.

Heat 2 tablespoons butter and 1 tablespoon oil in large skillet and brown beef rolls on all sides.

When browned, pour in bouillon and wine. Cover, turn heat to low, and simmer for 1 hour, until meat is tender.

Remove beef olives to serving platter.

Thicken sauce with flour and butter mixture. Pour over beef and sprinkle with parsley.

6 SERVINGS

Planked Eggplant

1 large eggplant	1 cup bread crumbs
2 tablespoons oil	1 small onion, grated
2 tablespoons butter	1 tablespoon tomato catsup
2 tablespoons flour	½ teaspoon ground cinnamon
1 cup milk	2 eggs, separated
1½ cups grated sharp Cheddar cheese	Salt to taste
	Freshly ground pepper

Preheat oven to 350°.

Do not peel eggplant. Cut in half lengthwise. With sharp spoon, scrape out centers, leaving ½-inch wall.

Chop pulp and saute in oil until tender.

Heat butter in large saucepan and add flour. Cook, stirring for 3 minutes. Add milk, and cook stirring until thick.

Add eggplant pulp, cheese, crumbs, onion, catsup, seasonings, and egg yolks. Remove from heat.

Beat whites until stiff and fold in. Fill eggplant shells with mixture.

Bake for 45-50 minutes, until puffy and firm.

6 SERVINGS

Shoofly Pie

The name Shoofly comes from the French Canadian *coufleur,* meaning cauliflower. The texture of the crumb surface should resemble a head of cauliflower.

½ teaspoon baking soda	1/8 teaspoon salt
½ cup boiling water	1/8 teaspoon nutmeg
1 cup maple syrup	⅓ cup shortening
1½ cups flour	9-inch pie shell, unbaked
½ cup brown sugar	

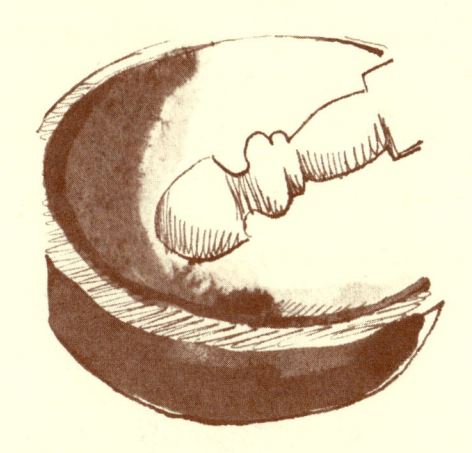

Preheat oven to 375°.

Dissolve soda in hot water. Add maple syrup and stir together.

In mixing bowl put flour, brown sugar, salt, and nutmeg. Cut shortening into flour mixture until texture is of coarse crumbs.

Pour one third the maple syrup mixture into pie shell. Add one third crumb mixture. Continue alternating layers of liquid and crumbs. Place last layer of crumbs on top.

Bake for 35 minutes.

6 SERVINGS

Vermont

Baked Bean Soup • 94
Carrot Soup • 95
Eggs Poached in Maple Syrup • 103
Scalloped Chicken • 100
Chicken Terrapin • 100
Dried Beef and Oyster Souffle • 90
New England Boiled Dinner • 101
Red Flannel Hash • 102
Sausage Pudding • 91
Ham Loaf • 92
Baked Beans • 93
New Corn Pudding • 96
Baked Apples and Onions • 102
Cinnamon Maple Toast • 104
Fried Cheesecakes • 104
Maple Custard Pie • 88
Maple Nut Upside-down Cake • 89
Honey Cake • 96
Molasses Rounds • 97
Pumpkin Pudding • 98
Fried Apple Pies • 99

Dear John:
I have missed your letters but this season is your busy time. A farmer's days are full ones, especially in Vermont where the growing season is short and the days' labors long. Molly must work with you and I am glad she is young and strong. To cook three times a day for 12 hands is only part of her chores. I hear the Spanish merino sheep are a good strain and their wool goes for a good price. Our weather hot and dry lately. Good for laying. Send me some news.

Affect.
Aunt Agnes

Dear Aunt Agnes:
You would like our Green Mountain state. Something like your native Scotland. We live simply but well. Our farm gives us all our provisions; maple aplenty for sweetening and the hands do like Molly's Maple Custard Pie and Maple Upside Down Cake.

Maple Custard Pie

This is a very sweet pie that will be especially liked by real maple lovers.

1 cup maple syrup	2 tablespoons butter
4 egg yolks	2 egg whites
⅓ cup milk	2 tablespoons sugar
2 tablespoons flour	1 baked 8-inch pie shell

In top of double boiler stir together the syrup, yolks, milk, and flour. Cook over hot water until thick and smooth, stirring frequently. Remove from heat, beat in butter, and cool.

Preheat oven to 350°.

Beat egg whites with sugar until stiff and shiny.

Pour custard mixture into pie shell. Cover with meringue.

Bake until meringue is lightly browned, about 12 minutes.

6 SERVINGS

Maple Nut Upside-Down Cake

1 cup maple syrup
½ cup walnuts, coarsely chopped
1 stick butter
1 cup sugar
2 eggs

½ teaspoon salt
2 teaspoons baking powder
1½ cups flour
½ cup milk
1 teaspoon vanilla

Preheat oven to 350°.
Grease a 9-inch square pan.
Pour in maple syrup and sprinkle with nuts.
In large mixing bowl cream butter until light, gradually adding sugar. Beat well.
Beat in eggs one at a time.
Mix dry ingredients together and add alternately with milk, mixing well.
Stir in vanilla.
Pour batter in pan and bake for 40 minutes, until cake tests done.
Remove from oven and let stand for 10 minutes.
Run knife around edges of pan and turn cake over onto large platter, allowing room for syrup to run over.

8 SERVINGS

"We make our cheese and when the oysters come into Will Hamlett's it makes a fair exchange. Molly makes a souffle from our own air dried smoked beef and oysters."

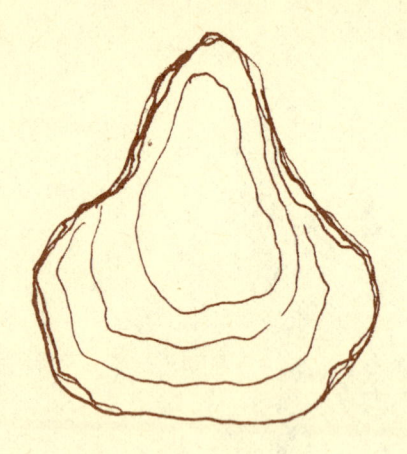

Dried Beef and Oyster Souffle

2 tablespoons butter
¼ pound air dried beef, shredded
2 tablespoons flour
½ teaspoon dry mustard
1 cup milk
4 egg yolks
Freshly ground pepper
Salt to taste
5 egg whites
1 cup oysters, drained and chopped

Preheat oven to 350°.

Melt butter in skillet and saute beef briefly. Stir in flour and mustard and cook 2 minutes. Pour in milk and cook, stirring, until thick and smooth.

Remove from heat and stir in yolks, one at a time. Season to taste. Stir in chopped oysters.

Beat whites until stiff and fold in.

Pour mixture into 1½-quart greased baking dish.

Bake for 30 minutes, until puffed and browned. Serve immediately.

4 SERVINGS

"Tis said there are still more sheep than people in Vermont but we are not lonely in our village. Wallis Carter very kind to help me with my smokehouse. All works fine and we produce some of the best hams in the area. Use corn cobs and maple sawdust for smoking. Our meat is mostly pork, some lamb. Molly uses our sausage in pudding and the ends of ham in loaves."

Sausage Pudding

1 pound sausage meat	¼ cup flour
1 sweet onion, peeled and sliced into thin rings	⅔ cup milk
2 eggs, separated	Salt to taste

Preheat oven to 425°.

In large skillet crumble sausage meat and cook over medium heat until pink has disappeared.

Remove sausage meat to 1½-quart shallow casserole.

In remaining fat, saute onion rings until soft. Put onion rings over sausage in casserole.

In bowl, beat together the egg yolks, flour, and milk. Add salt and pepper and fold in stiffly beaten whites. Pour mixture over sausage and onions.

Bake for 14 minutes, until puffed and firm.

NOTE: Two medium apples, pared, cored, and sliced, can replace the onion rings.

4 TO 5 SERVINGS

Ham Loaf

2 pounds ground ham
1 medium apple, peeled and chopped
1 medium onion, minced
2 teaspoons mustard
1 tablespoon brown sugar or maple sugar
1 egg
2 tablespoons chopped parsley
1 cup dry bread crumbs

Preheat oven to 350°.
Put all ingredients in large bowl and mix well with hands. Shape into loaf and put into baking pan.
Bake for 1 hour.
Serve hot or cold with mustard, green tomato pickle, or chutney.

6 SERVINGS

"A large garden and orchard gives us all we need for our year's supplies and the beans are plentiful to bake every Saturday with enough for soup for breakfast."

Baked Beans

  2 pounds dried yellow-eyed beans   1 teaspoon dry mustard
2/3 cup maple syrup (1 cup of   1/2 teaspoon ginger
    brown sugar can be   1/2 pound lean salt pork
    substituted)

Soak beans in water overnight. Drain off water.
In 4-quart bean pot add fresh water to cover beans.
Preheat oven to 375°.
Stir maple syrup, mustard, and ginger into beans.
Slice rind of salt pork about every 1/4-inch and place, lean side down, on top of beans with rind up. Press down into beans a bit.
    Cover and bake for several hours (about 6) until beans are soft, adding water as needed to cover beans. Toward end of baking, allow sauce to thicken by not adding water.

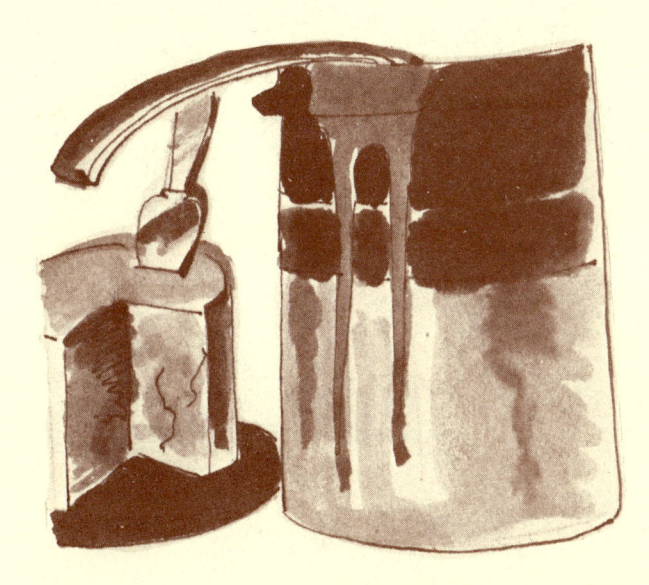

8 SERVINGS

Baked Bean Soup

2 cups leftover baked beans, including liquid	2 cups canned tomatoes, drained and sieved
4 cups water	Salt to taste
½ large onion, peeled and diced	Freshly ground pepper
2 stalks celery, chopped	

Put beans, water, onion, and celery in large saucepan. Bring to a boil. Cover and simmer for 1 hour.

Put mixture through food mill.

Return to pan and add tomatoes and seasonings to taste. Simmer for 40 minutes.

Remove from heat and let stand 3 to 4 hours.

Reheat slowly and correct seasonings.

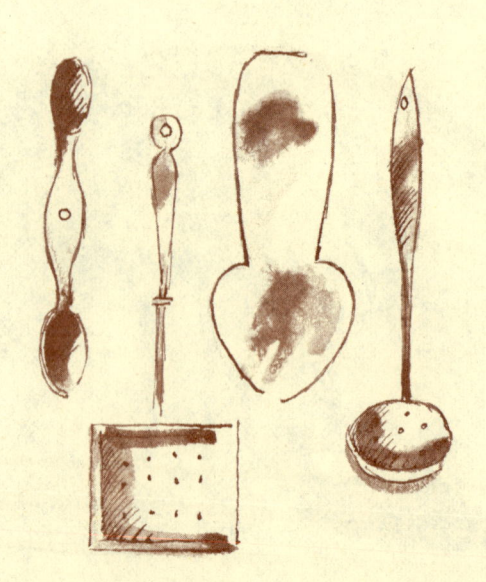

6 SERVINGS

Dear John:

Our garden producing carrots now. They make a good soup for early Fall with the leeks. Stopped over at Mrs. Foote's for dinner after meeting and she had her green corn pudding. I had given her one of your hams for the wedding and it went well. A honey cake and molasses rounds made enough for all.

Carrot Soup

1 tablespoon butter
1 leek, white part only, chopped fine
8 carrots, peeled and grated
1 small potato, peeled and diced
6 cups chicken broth
Salt to taste
Freshly ground pepper
1 teaspoon sugar
1½ cups rich milk

In large saucepan heat butter. Add leek and saute for 5 minutes.
Add grated carrots, potato, broth, and seasonings. Bring to a boil. Cover, turn heat down, and simmer for 45 minutes.
Puree in blender.
Return to pan and add milk. Serve very hot.

6 SERVINGS

New Corn Pudding

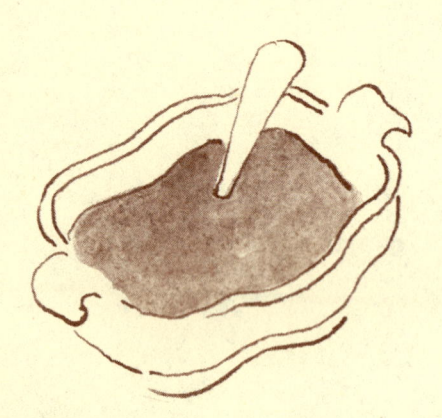

This recipe was given to me by Mrs. E. H. Foote's daughter-in-law, Mrs. Richard Foote.

24 ears of new corn	2 tablespoons melted butter
Milk	1 teaspoon salt
3 eggs, well beaten	4 tablespoons sugar

Preheat oven to 250°.
With sharp knife point, cut down each row of corn kernels. With back of knife or spoon, scrape milk from kernels into bowl. Amount of milk depends on the corn.
Add eggs, milk, butter, salt, and sugar. Mixture should be consistency of corn bread batter, so add milk until it seems right. There will be about 4 cups of pudding.
Pour into greased shallow baking pan.
Bake 2 to 3 hours, until set, brown, and quite dry. Cut into squares.

6 TO 8 SERVINGS

Honey Cake

½ cup butter	½ teaspoon nutmeg
3 eggs, separated	¼ teaspoon allspice
1 cup honey	½ teaspoon salt
4 cups flour	1 teaspoon baking soda
½ teaspoon cinnamon	1 cup water
½ teaspoon ginger	1 cup chopped nuts

Preheat oven to 350°.
Cream together butter and egg yolks. Add honey and mix well.

Mix together dry ingredients and add alternately with water, blending well.

Beat whites until stiff and fold into batter. Stir in nuts.

Bake in two 7 x 3 x 2-inch loaf pans for 45 to 50 minutes. Cool on racks.

Frost with a lemon icing.

YIELD: 2 LOAVES

Molasses Rounds

½ cup melted butter
1 cup molasses
1 tablespoon ginger

1 teaspoon baking soda
2 tablespoons sour cream
3½ cups flour

Combine in large bowl the butter, molasses, and ginger.

Dissolve soda in sour cream and stir in.

Beat in flour with wooden spoon. Dough should be fairly stiff, to roll, not sticky. Chill.

Preheat oven to 350°.

Roll out on floured board to ¼-inch thickness. Cut into 2-inch rounds.

Place on lightly greased cookie sheet and bake for 10 minutes.

YIELD: ABOUT 36

Dear Aunt Agnes:

Yes, our sidewalks are made of marble, where we have them. You would have enjoyed Molly's quilting bee last evening. Many ladies sewing and talking and eating pumpkin puddings and fried apple pies with our first cider. Our summer is past and we must think of provisioning for the long winter ahead. We have killed some of the old hens and they make good Scalloped Chicken or Terrapin.

Pumpkin Pudding

This is a nice change from pie and slightly less caloric.

2 tablespoons soft butter
½ cup brown sugar or maple sugar
1½ cups cooked, strained pumpkin
3 eggs
2 cups rich milk

2 tablespoons rum
½ cup sugar
1 teaspoon cinnamon
½ teaspoon ginger
½ teaspoon nutmeg
¼ teaspoon salt

Preheat oven to 350°.
Spread butter around bottom and sides of 1½-quart baking dish. Sprinkle brown sugar over butter.
In bowl mix together all other ingredients, blending well. Pour into baking dish. Set dish in pan of hot water.
Bake for 1 hour, until set.
Serve cold with cream.

6 SERVINGS

Fried Apple Pies

We like a thick, well-spiced apple butter as filling but a flavorful applesauce will do very well.

    2 cups flour
    ½ teaspoon salt
    4 tablespoons butter
½ to ¾ cup light cream
Thick applesauce or apple butter
Powdered sugar

In large bowl put flour, salt, and butter. Cut butter into flour until well mixed. Add cream gradually until a soft dough is formed. Dough should not be sticky.

Roll out on floured board about ¼-inch thick. Cut into circles, using a saucer as a guide.

Spread each circle with 1 to 2 tablespoons applesauce or apple butter. Fold circles over to make half-moons and pinch together on edges with fork.

Heat deep fat to 370°.

Fry pies one at a time until golden and crispy. Sprinkle with sugar while warm.

YIELD: 6 TO 8 PIES

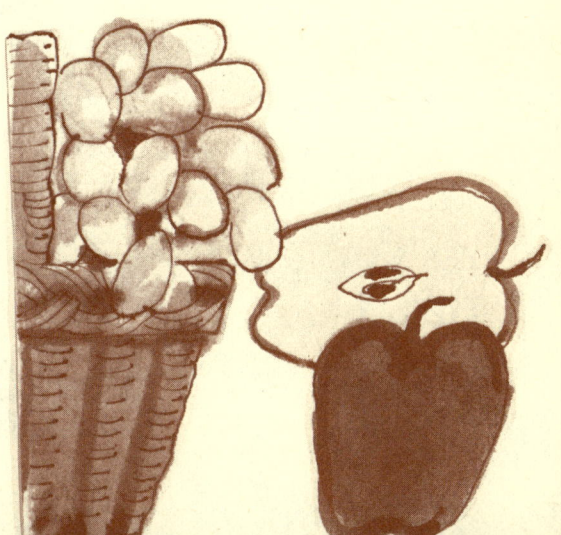

Scalloped Chicken

5 pound fowl
1 onion stuck with 6 cloves
1 large carrot
1 stalk celery with leaves
10 peppercorns
2 cups plain bread or corn bread dressing
6 tablespoons butter
6 tablespoons flour
Salt to taste
1 teaspoon paprika
½ teaspoon nutmeg

Put chicken, onion, carrot, celery, and peppercorns in large kettle. Cover with cold water. Bring to a boil, skimming. Reduce heat, cover, and simmer for 1½ hours, until chicken is tender. Cool.

Remove meat from bones in large pieces.

Boil broth at high heat until reduced to 3 cups.

Preheat oven to 350°.

In saucepan melt butter and stir in flour. Cook for 2 minutes. Pour in broth and cook, stirring, until thick and smooth. Season with salt, paprika, and nutmeg.

In large shallow baking dish spread 1½ cups bread dressing. Place pieces of chicken over dressing. Pour sauce over all. Sprinkle remaining dressing over top.

Bake for 30 minutes, until bubbling.

8 SERVINGS

Chicken Terrapin

2 cups diced cooked chicken
2 hard-boiled eggs, chopped
Juice of 1 lemon
2 tablespoons butter
3 tablespoons flour
2 cups milk
1 teaspoon nutmeg
Salt to taste
Toast

In bowl combine chicken, eggs, and lemon juice.

In saucepan heat butter, add flour, and cook for 2 minutes. Add milk and cook, stirring, until thick and smooth. Add seasonings.

Combine chicken mixture and sauce and serve over hot toast.

4 SERVINGS

"The cold cellar keeps all we need for my favorite boiled dinner; Molly says I like the hash that comes after, best. Our apple trees produce good keepers, especially the Wealthy and Sheepnose. They bake well with the sweet onion."

New England Boiled Dinner

4 pound piece of beef round or brisket of corned beef
½ pound salt pork
4 turnips peeled and quartered
1 cabbage, quartered and cored
6 carrots, peeled and quartered
8 onions, peeled
6 potatoes, peeled
8 beets
Fresh grated horseradish
Pickles

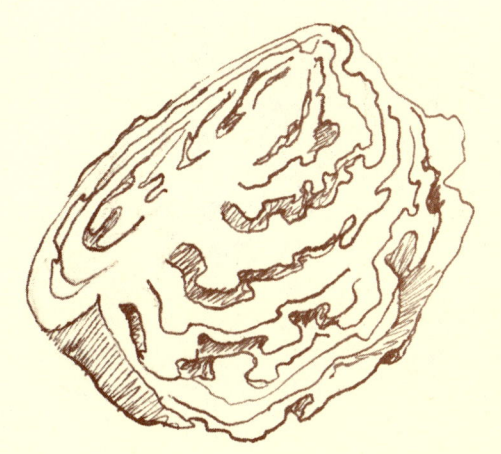

Place beef in large kettle and cover with water. Bring to a boil and simmer, covered, for 2 hours.

Add salt pork and simmer for 1 hour.

Add turnips, cabbage and carrots. Simmer for 1 hour. Add onions and potatoes and cook 30 minutes longer, until all vegetables and meat are tender.

Cook beets separately.

Remove meat from broth and slice on large platter. Surround with vegetables.

Serve with fresh grated horseradish and pickles.

8 SERVINGS

Red Flannel Hash

1/8 pound salt pork diced small	2 cups chopped boiled potatoes
1 cup chopped corned beef	Salt to taste
1 cup chopped cooked beets	Freshly ground pepper

In large skillet cook pork until crisp.

Combine other ingredients carefully and spread over bottom of skillet. Cook over medium heat until a crust forms on bottom.

NOTE: Each ingredient should be chopped separately, never ground.

4 SERVINGS

Baked Apples and Onions

An excellent accompaniment to ham, sausage, or pork chops.

8 tart apples, pared, cored, and sliced into rings.	Freshly ground pepper
	2 tablespoons sugar
2 large sweet onions, peeled and sliced into thin rings	½ cup cracker crumbs tossed in 2 tablespoons butter
2 tablespoons butter	½ cup hot water
Salt to taste	

Preheat oven to 350°.
Butter a deep 2-quart baking dish.
Arrange half the apple slices in bottom of dish. Cover with half the onions. Dot with 1 tablespoon butter and sprinkle with half the seasonings. Repeat layers.
Sprinkle crumbs over top and pour in hot water.
Cover and bake for 1 to 1½ hours, until tender.

6 SERVINGS

"Glad you like our syrup. A Vermont receipt we both like is eggs cooked in maple syrup. Also cinnamon maple toast with hot cider. Molly sends her love and her own receipt for Fried Cheesecake to have with our pork tenderloin."

Eggs Poached in Maple Syrup

Do try this recipe. It is remarkably good and tastes like superb French Toast.

½ cup maple syrup   4 thick slices buttered toast
4 eggs

Pour syrup into skillet and bring to a boil.
Slide eggs into pan one at a time and turn heat to simmer. Cook eggs, basting with syrup, until yolks are firm and whites are opaque.
Lift eggs onto slices of toast and pour remaining syrup over them.

4 SERVINGS

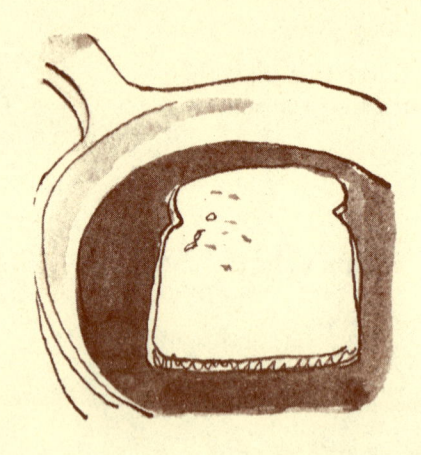

Cinnamon Maple Toast

This is a wonderful after-school snack or simple dessert.

Thick-sliced firm bread, 1 slice per person
Soft butter
Maple sugar
Cinnamon
Chopped walnuts, butternuts, or pecans

Toast bread slices on one side.
Spread untoasted sides with butter, sprinkle with sugar, a dusting of cinnamon and nuts.
Place slices on baking sheet and put under broiler. Broil until sugar is melted and bubbly.

Fried Cheesecakes
(From Yankee Hill Country Cooking by Beatrice Vaughn)

1 cup grated Cheddar cheese
2½ tablespoons flour
½ teaspoon grated lemon rind
Pinch of pepper
⅔ cup sour cream
3 egg yolks, beaten

In large bowl combine cheese, flour, and seasonings. Mix in sour cream and yolks.

Heat a lightly greased griddle.

Drop batter onto griddle in small spoonfuls. When bubbles appear on upper sides of cakes, turn and brown on other side.

These cakes are very light and should be handled gently.

6 SERVINGS

Maine

Pea Soup • 116
Main Corn Chowder • 117
Smoked Fish Chowder • 122
Shrimp Soup • 115
Lobster Stew • 116
Baked Bluefish • 110
Stewed Mussels • 113
Baked Maine Smelts • 114
Sauteed Scallops • 118
Chicken Stew • 118
Rabbit Pie • 121
Spiced Beef • 114
Bean Pot Stew • 120
Blueberry Pancakes • 111
Doughnuts • 122
Rhubarb Pie • 109
Blueberry Cake • 111
Blueberry Pudding • 112
Blueberry Slump • 112
Lobster Cake • 123
Snickerdoodles • 124
Carrot Cookies • 124
Sweet Cream Cake • 125

Dear Mary:

Your wedding was a pretty sight and Peter a fond young man. We will all miss you, and Maine so far away, but he must go where his trade takes him and most of our ships are built in Maine. I am sending my best receipts for the berries and dishes you want. Don't forget to cut the rhubarb into small dice for the pie. It seems to do best that way. You have much food from the sea and you must learn to use it well. Bluefish can be done with herbs and salt pork . . . .

Rhubarb Pie

8-inch pie shell, prebaked 10 minutes	¼ cup flour
½ cup ground almonds	2 eggs, separated
1 tablespoon butter	1 cup milk
¾ cup sugar	½ teaspoon nutmeg
	1 cup rhubarb, cut in ½-inch dice

Preheat oven to 350°.

Sprinkle ground almonds in bottom of pie shell.

In bowl cream together the butter and sugar. Add flour alternately with milk. Beat in yolks and nutmeg.

Beat whites until soft peaks form and fold into yolk mixture. Fold in rhubarb.

Pour into pie shell and bake for 40 minutes, until set.

Cool to room temperature before cutting.

6 SERVINGS

Baked Bluefish

1 Bluefish, cleaned, with gills removed, head and tail left on	Dill
¼ pound salt pork	Chives
Parsley	Salt to taste
	Freshly ground pepper

Preheat oven to 400°.

Measure fish at its thickest part through with a ruler. This determines the cooking time. Allow 10 minutes for each inch.

Stuff cavity of fish with any or all of the herbs. Season.

Place fish in baking pan and put strips of salt pork over top.

Bake for required length of time. Test for doneness by inserting tines of fork in thickest part. If flesh separates easily, fish is done.

NOTE: This seems as good a place as any to mention the problem of salt pork. It was used extensively in colonial times and, very often, as an entree. Unfortunately, today we do not get the nice lean salt pork that our forefathers had. They butchered their own pigs and we are dependent on commercial meat packers who send out salt pork that is solid white fat with nary a scrap of lean on it. Occasionally, with diligent searching, it is possible to find some of the old-fashioned kind. You may prefer to use thick slices of well-smoked bacon instead. Bacon ends are an excellent substitute.

Dear Aunt Agnes:
  The receipt book here safely and in time for our blueberries. Peter greatly enjoys your cake and we have pancakes and puddings of this wild berry that grows everywhere.

Blueberry Cake

½ cup butter or margarine
1 cup sugar
2 eggs, separated
1½ cups flour
1 teaspoon baking powder
⅓ cup milk
¼ teaspoon salt
1 teaspoon vanilla
1½ cups fresh blueberries lightly sprinkled with flour

Preheat oven to 350°.
Cream butter and ¾ cup sugar until light. Beat in yolks, mixing well.
Combine dry ingredients and add alternately to batter with milk. Add vanilla.
Beat whites until stiff with remaining ¼ cup sugar. Fold in berries.
Pour batter into 9-inch square greased pan.
Bake for 45 to 50 minutes, until done.

8 SERVINGS

Blueberry Pancakes

1 cup flour
1 teaspoon baking powder
½ teaspoon salt
1 teaspoon sugar
2 tablespoons melted butter
1 egg
Buttermilk
1 cup blueberries

In bowl combine dry ingredients. Stir in butter, egg, blueberries, and enough buttermilk to make a batter that drips off the spoon.
Heat lightly greased griddle and drop batter by spoonfuls. When bubbles appear, turn and brown on other side.
Serve immediately with warm butter and maple syrup.
NOTE: We like our pancakes thin, but people have very definite ideas on the subject, so make the batter the consistency *you* like.

YIELD: 12 PANCAKES

Blueberry Pudding

I tried an old recipe for a steamed blueberry pudding but found it much too doughy for our tastes today. This simpler version does more for the berries and fits our modern diets.

3 cups blueberries
¾ cup brown sugar
½ teaspoon mace

⅓ cup butter
¾ cup flour

Preheat oven to 350°.
Butter a 1-quart baking dish. Put berries in bottom. Sprinkle over berries half of brown sugar and mace. Put remaining sugar, butter, and flour in bowl and work together until a crumbly mixture is formed. Spread over top of berries.
Bake for 40 minutes.
Serve at room temperature with cream.

4 TO 5 SERVINGS

Blueberry Slump

2 cups blueberries
½ cup sugar
1 cup water
1 cup flour

2 teaspoons baking powder
¼ teaspoon salt
¼ to ½ cup buttermilk

Put berries, sugar, and water in saucepan. Bring to a boil and stew until berries are soft.
Place dry ingredients in bowl and add milk to make a soft dough.
Drop by spoonfuls into boiling blueberry sauce. Cover and cook until dumplings are firm and cooked through, 10 to 20 minutes.

4 TO 6 SERVINGS

"Lobsters of a large size to make a full pot of stew. Mussels, smelts, cod, food from the sea and land to keep us well. Truly one of God's most favored countries."

Stewed Mussels

4 dozen mussels   1 blade mace
1 bay leaf

Scrub mussels well and beard them. Place in large kettle with ½-inch water in bottom. Add bay leaf and mace.

Cover and cook over high heat until shells open. Continue steaming for 5 minutes. Serve with melted butter.

4 SERVINGS

Spiced Beef

"We sent one of Peter's friends our recipe for lobster stew and in return his wife showed me her method of preparing spiced beef."

4 pound piece beef round	Freshly ground pepper
Flour	1-inch stick cinnamon
2 tablespoons fat	1 cup water
6 cloves	½ cup cider vinegar
2 onions, chopped	3 large potatoes, peeled and
2 carrots, chopped	sliced thin
Salt to taste	

Dredge meat lightly with flour.

Heat fat in heavy Dutch oven or casserole. Brown meat on all sides over medium-high heat.

Remove meat from pan and stick with whole cloves. Put carrots and onions in bottom of pan. Replace meat and sprinkle with salt and pepper. Add cinnamon, water, and vinegar. Cover and simmer for 3 hours.

Add potatoes and cook 30 minutes longer.

NOTE: Meat can be cooked at 275° oven instead of on burner.

6 TO 8 SERVINGS

"When the smelts run we all go to the sea for them. I find them best baked with our salt pork."

Baked Maine Smelts

The amounts given are indefinite. The two ingredients are smelts and salt pork (if lean). Otherwise use bacon.

Preheat oven to 400°.

In flat baking tin interweave the smelts with slices of pork or bacon, much as if you were weaving a basket.

Bake for 10 to 15 minutes, until smelts and bacon are molded into a crisp cake.

This is worth experimenting with when the smelts are running.

"The shrimp here are very small but very sweet and when we net them and make a soup with the new potatoes and peas it is a fine meal."

Shrimp Soup

1 medium onion, chopped
2 tablespoons butter
2 tablespoons flour
4 cups milk
1 pound Maine shrimp, cooked, cleaned, and deveined
1 cup fresh or frozen tiny peas
12 tiny new potatoes or 6 large ones, quartered
1 cup hot cream
Salt to taste
Freshly ground pepper

In top of large double boiler heat butter and saute onion until soft. Stir in flour and cook for 2 minutes. Add milk and cook, stirring, for 5 minutes.

Add shrimp, peas, and potatoes. Cook over hot water for 20 to 30 minutes.

Add hot cream and season to taste.

4 TO 5 SERVINGS

Lobster Stew

An interesting historical note is that the very early settlers did not appreciate these huge lobsters at all. They were much too used to their "Pease porridge" diet and the shellfish did not satisfy them. However, they eventually learned to acclimate their eating habits to New England provender.

3 1¼ pound lobsters
½ cup butter
1 quart rich milk

Steam the live lobsters in a small amount of water for 20 minutes.
Let cool and, as soon as you can handle them, remove the meat and cut into bite-size pieces. Save the fat, tomalley, and coral.
In a heavy kettle heat the butter. Simmer the fat, tomalley, and coral for 7 or 8 minutes. Add the pieces of lobster meat and cook over low heat for 10 minutes. Very slowly, pour in the milk, stirring constantly. Remove from heat. Cool and refrigerate.
Let age at least 12 hours (some recommend 24). Reheat without boiling.

3 TO 4 SERVINGS

Pea Soup

This recipe is from the files of our friend Knud Anderson.

2 cups green split peas
4 quarts water
½ ham bone
3 medium carrots, chopped
2 celery stalks, chopped
2 medium onions, chopped
1/8 teaspoon thyme
Salt to taste

Rinse peas well and soak in 1 quart water overnight. Do not discard water but add 3 quarts more water and ham bone. Bring to a boil and skim top. Simmer for one hour over low heat. Add vegetables and thyme and simmer for one hour longer. Remove bone. Press soup through sieve or put through food mill. Reheat, season and serve.

8 TO 10 SERVINGS

Dear Mary:

We have the first of our corn and it won't be long before yours will come. Don't forget Cousin Hannah's chowder, good to fill up your young man. You did not mention scallops but there must be plenty and they go nicely in chowder or sauteed in the pan. How I wish I could see your beautiful state but traveling that far, with the many disruptions on the roads, is very difficult for me.

Maine Corn Chowder
(From The Yankee Cookbook, by Imogene Wolcott)

3 tablespoons fat salt pork diced
1 onion, sliced
2 potatoes, diced
1½ cups boiling water
1 cup fresh or frozen corn kernels
1 cup milk
1 cup cream
Salt to taste
Freshly ground pepper
4 common crackers, split

Fry out salt pork in skillet. Add onion and cook until golden brown. Add potatoes, water, and corn and cook until potatoes are tender.
Add milk and cream and reheat. Season.
Place a cracker in each soup bowl and pour chowder over.

4 SERVINGS

Sauteed Scallops

1 pint scallops; if large, cut in halves
Flour
4 tablespoons butter
Salt to taste
Freshly ground pepper
2 tablespoons minced parsley

In large skillet heat butter to almost smoking. Flour scallops lightly and put in pan. Keep turning with a spatula to brown them on all sides. They should be cooked quickly at high heat so they will remain tender and the flour will not absorb the fat.

Season to taste and sprinkle with parsley.

4 SERVINGS

Dear Aunt Agnes:
 The people of Maine are strong and bold of character. It is not an easy life. They say a Maine man lives well with one foot in the sea and the other on land. 'Tis true we must eat hearty to survive on this rugged coast. Stews of chicken and beef and pies of game which we have in plenty.

Chicken Stew
(From The Yankee Cookbook by Imogene Wolcott)

These stews and chowders have a certain sameness to the ingredients, as did most of the colonial food, especially that of the northern New England states. However, their ingredients were absolutely fresh and the flavors outstanding. Chickens were not the frozen mass produced kind we have today and therefore a very good stew could be made with just cold water and a minimum of seasoning added to the fresh-killed bird.

2 3½ to 4 pound chickens (fresh, if possible)
6 potatoes, pared and sliced
3 onions, peeled and sliced
Cold water
2 tablespoons butter
1 cup rich milk or half and half
Salt to taste
Freshly ground pepper
3 tablespoons minced parsley
6 to 8 common crackers

Cut chicken for stewing. In a large kettle place alternate layers of chicken, slices of potato, and thinly sliced onion. Cover with cold water. Simmer gently until chicken is tender. (Allow about 1 hour.)

Add butter in small bits and milk. Season and add parsley.

Split crackers, moisten in milk, and reheat in stew.

8 SERVINGS

Bean Pot Stew

It is interesting to note that we are going back to the grass-fed rather than corn-fed beef and these early recipes will be helpful in showing us how to cook our meats more slowly and for longer hours to make them tender.

2 pounds beef round, well trimmed and cut into 1-inch cubes	4 tablespoons regular oats
	Salt to taste
	Freshly ground pepper
1 onion, sliced	½ teaspoon thyme
4 carrots, diced	1 tablespoon minced parsley
1 medium turnip, diced	Water
2 parsnips, diced	4 large potatoes, peeled and diced

Preheat oven to 300°.

In large bean pot or heavy casserole put cubed beef and onion. Cover pot and cook in oven for 45 minutes.

Remove from oven and add all ingredients except potatoes. Add cold water to cover. Cook for 2½ to 3 hours, until meat is tender.

Add potatoes and cook for 30 minutes, until tender.

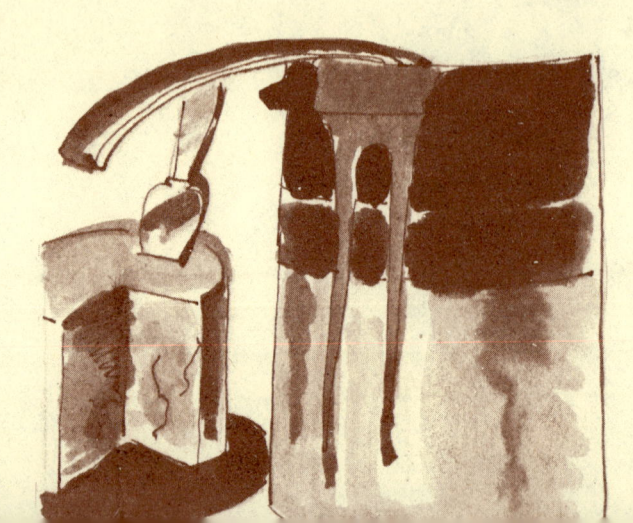

6 SERVINGS

Rabbit Pie

1 rabbit, skinned, cleaned, and cut into pieces
1 stalk celery
1 carrot
1 onion
1 bay leaf
½ teaspoon thyme
Pinch of rosemary
3 sprigs parsley
Salt to taste
6 peppercorns
1 shallot, chopped
1 tablespoon bacon fat
2 tablespoons butter
3 tablespoons flour
2 cups broth
4 carrots, diced and cooked until tender
2 tablespoons chopped parsley
½ pound bacon, cooked and chopped
1 recipe basic pastry

In large kettle put rabbit pieces, celery, carrot, onion, bay leaf, thyme, rosemary, parsley sprigs, salt, peppercorns, shallot, and water to cover. Bring to a boil, skimming if necessary. Cover and reduce heat. Simmer until tender, about 1 hour or more.

Remove rabbit and take meat from bones. Cut into ¾-inch dice.

Strain broth and reduce over high heat until 2 cups remain.

In saucepan melt bacon fat and butter and add flour. Cook for 2 minutes. Add broth and cook, stirring, until thickened and smooth.

Add rabbit and cooked carrots to sauce.

Grease a shallow 1 or 1½ quart baking dish. The size depends on how much rabbit there is but you should have at least 2 cups.

Spread rabbit and sauce over bottom of dish. Sprinkle parsley and chopped bacon on top. Cover with pastry crust, sealing edges. Refrigerate for 1 hour.

Preheat oven to 400°.

For golden crust, brush pastry with egg yolk beaten with cream.

Bake for 30 minutes, until browned.

4 SERVINGS

Smoked Fish Chowder

¼ pound salt pork, diced
1 large onion, sliced
4 medium potatoes, peeled and sliced
Water
Salt to taste
Freshly ground pepper
1 bay leaf
5 cups milk
1½ pounds finnan haddie cut into 1-inch pieces

In large saucepan, brown pork. Add onion and saute until soft.
Add potatoes and water to cover. Add salt, pepper, and bay leaf. Cover and simmer until potatoes are barely tender.
Add milk and fish and simmer 15 to 20 minutes.

6 SERVINGS

"I have learned a new task, making rugs with a hook. We use our own wools and dyes of butternut, onion skins and beetroot. Hannah Morse taught me and it is enjoyable and social during these wintry days. Her children make popcorn balls for the tree which we will all share over the holiday. We fry doughnuts and enjoy a cake called Lobster Cake; there seems to be no reason for the name. I shall give them your Snickerdoodles, Carrot Cookies and my Sweet Cream Cake. A Happy Christmas and we shall miss being with you but it shall be a good time in this lovely country."

Doughnuts

3 eggs
1 cup sugar
4 tablespoons butter, melted
3 teaspoons baking powder
1 cup milk
1 teaspoon salt
1 teaspoon nutmeg
3 cups flour (about)

In large bowl beat eggs and add sugar and butter.

Beat in dry ingredients, using enough flour to make dough soft enough to handle, not sticky.

Roll out and cut with doughnut cutter.

Fry in fat heated to 360°. Roll in sugar while hot. (Optional)

Lobster Cake

1 cup butter
2 cups sugar
4 eggs
3 cups flour
¾ teaspoon cream of tartar
½ teaspoon baking soda
½ teaspoon salt
1 cup milk

1 cup molasses
½ teaspoon ground cloves
½ teaspoon cinnamon
½ teaspoon nutmeg
¼ teaspoon ginger
½ cup chopped raisins
½ cup chopped citron

Preheat oven to 350°.

In mixing bowl cream butter and add sugar gradually, beating until light.

Add eggs one at a time.

Mix flour, cream of tartar, soda, and salt together. Add alternately to batter with milk.

Divide batter into two bowls. To one bowl add molasses and spices. To other bowl add raisins and citron.

Put by spoonfuls into two greased 9 x 5-inch loaf pans, alternating mixtures to get a marbleized effect.

Bake for 1 hour, until done.

12 TO 14 SERVINGS

Snickerdoodles

½ cup butter
1 cup sugar
1 egg
2 cups flour
2 teaspoons baking powder
½ cup milk
1 teaspoon vanilla
Cinnamon-sugar

Preheat oven to 375°.
In mixing bowl cream together the butter and sugar until light. Beat in egg.
Mix together the flour and baking powder and stir in.
Add milk and vanilla and beat batter until well mixed.
Drop by spoonfuls onto greased baking sheet. Sprinkle with cinnamon-sugar.
Bake for 10 minutes.

YIELD: ABOUT 36

Carrot Cookies

⅓ cup butter or margarine
1 cup sugar
2 eggs
1 teaspoon vanilla
Grated rind of 1 orange
1 cup very finely grated raw carrots
2½ cups flour
1 tablespoon baking powder
¼ teaspoon salt
¼ teaspoon ginger
½ teaspoon nutmeg
½ cup chopped dates
½ cup chopped nuts

Preheat oven to 375°.
In mixing bowl cream butter and sugar until light. Beat in eggs. Add vanilla, orange rind, and carrots. Mix well.
Mix dry ingredients together and add with dates and nuts. Blend well.

Drop by teaspoonfuls onto greased baking sheet.
Bake for 12 minutes.

                        YIELD: 48 COOKIES

Sweet Cream Cake

2 eggs, separated
½ cup white sugar
½ cup brown sugar
1 cup heavy cream
2 cups flour
¼ teaspoon salt

2 teaspoons cream of tartar
1 teaspoon baking soda
1 teaspoon vanilla or rum
½ cup chopped walnuts
½ cup whipped cream

Preheat oven to 375°.
In mixing bowl beat yolks, adding sugars gradually.
Mix dry ingredients together and add to yolks alternately with cream. Stir in vanilla and nuts.
Beat whites until stiff and fold into batter.
Divide batter evenly between 2 greased 8-inch layer cake tins.
Bake for 25 to 30 minutes, until cake tests done.
Turn layers out onto racks and cool.
Put together with ½ cup whipped cream between layers and frost top and sides with butter and sugar frosting.

Butter and Sugar Frosting

¼ cup butter
1½ cups confectioners' sugar

2 egg whites
1 teaspoon vanilla

In mixing bowl cream together the butter and ½ cup sugar.
Beat egg whites until stiff, gradually beating in 1 cup sugar.
Combine mixtures and beat together until smooth and frosting is thick enough to hold shape. Beat in vanilla.

Menus

WE have suggested menus for each state, placing dishes in categories for special occasions. You might like to put together some menus yourself, picking out recipes that particularly appeal to you.

Dinner in Connecticut

Boiled Chicken with Oyster Sauce
Corner Biscuits
Scalloped Onions
Pumpkin Pudding

•

Christmas Tea in Massachusetts

Gingerbread
Shrewsbury Cakes
Chocolate Puffs
Upside-Down Apple Tart

•

Rhode Island Brunch

Kedgeree
Jonnycake with Dried Beef Sauce
Peach Pan Dowdy

New Hampshire Summer Picnic

*Cream of Green Pea Soup
Grilled Trout
Fried Potato Cakes
Washington Pie*

•

Vermont Buffet

*Ham Loaf
Corn Pudding
Baked Apples and Onions
Maple Nut Upside-Down Cake*

•

Sunday Night Supper in Maine

*Lobster Stew
Blueberry Pudding*

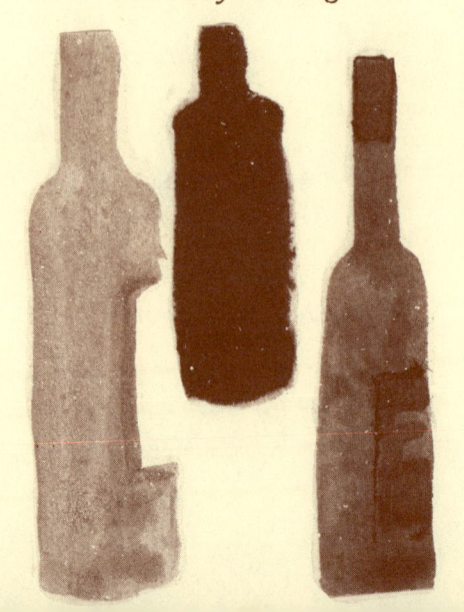

Recipes from Harrington's Kitchen

THE following are recipes created in Harrington's kitchens for their products. They were chosen, and are presented here, because of the enthusiasm with which they have been received by Harrington's customers.

Ham and Cheese Puff Ring

4 tablespoons butter
1 cup beer or ale
½ teaspoon salt
1 cup flour
4 eggs
1 cup grated sharp Cheddar cheese
1 cup ground ham

Preheat oven to 375°.

In saucepan over high heat bring butter, beer, and salt to a full boil. With wooden spoon beat in flour, stirring rapidly over heat for about 2 minutes until a smooth ball is formed and a light film forms on bottom of pan. Remove from heat.

Beat in eggs one at a time, either by hand or with mixer. Make sure each egg is thoroughly incorporated before adding the next one.

In greased 10-inch round dish or pie pan, spread a circle of half the dough. Sprinkle 1 cup ham and ½ cup cheese over this circle. Cover with other half dough. Sprinkle remaining cheese over top.

Bake for 45 minutes, until puffed and brown.

4 SERVINGS

Ham and Asparagus Casserole

1½ pounds asparagus, cooked until tender but still firm
2 cups diced ham
3 tablespoons flour
3 tablespoons butter or margarine
1½ cups milk
½ cup sour cream
Juice of ½ lemon
Salt to taste
Freshly ground pepper
½ teaspoon curry powder
½ cup buttered bread or cracker crumbs

Preheat oven to 350°.
In shallow baking dish place asparagus spears. Put ham over asparagus.
In saucepan heat butter and stir in flour. Cook for 2 minutes. Add milk and cook, stirring until thick and smooth.
Remove from heat and blend in sour cream and seasonings. Pour over asparagus mixture in baking dish. Sprinkle crumbs over top.
Bake for 20 minutes, until heated through.

4 SERVINGS

Corn Muffins with Bacon

4 strips bacon, cooked crisp and crumbled
1 cup yellow corn meal
1 cup flour
⅓ cup sugar
3 teaspoons baking powder
½ teaspoon salt
1 egg
1 cup milk
¼ cup bacon fat

Preheat oven to 400°.
In large bowl place all dry ingredients. Quickly stir in egg, milk, and bacon fat. Mix well, Stir in bacon.
Fill greased muffin tins with batter.
Bake for 20 minutes.

YIELD: 12 MUFFINS

Spinach Salad with Bacon Dressing

1 pound fresh spinach leaves,
4 to 6 slices bacon
1 tablespoon brown sugar
Salt to taste
Freshly ground pepper
¼ cup cider vinegar
1 tablespoon chopped scallions
1 hard-boiled egg yolk, sieved

Fry bacon slices until crisp. Remove from pan and drain. Pour off all but 3 tablespoons bacon fat.

Put spinach leaves in large salad bowl.

Put skillet with remaining fat over medium heat. Stir in brown sugar, salt and pepper. Add vinegar and bring to a boil.

Pour over spinach and toss well.

Add scallions, egg yolk, and crumbled bacon. Toss again and serve.

6 SERVINGS

Dried Beef Chowder

⅓ cup chopped onion
2 tablespoons butter or margarine
3 medium potatoes, peeled and diced
1 cup water
1 cup sliced dried beef
2 cups cream style corn
1 cup milk
Salt to taste
Freshly ground pepper

Cook onion in margarine until transparent. Add potatoes, beef, and water.

Cover and simmer until potatoes are tender, about 15 minutes.

Stir in corn and milk. Season to taste with salt and pepper.

Return to boiling before serving.

5 SERVINGS

Ham Souffle

1 cup ground ham
3 tablespoons butter or margarine
3 tablespoons flour
1 cup milk
½ cup grated Cheddar cheese
½ teaspoon salt
¼ teaspoon dry mustard
1 teaspoon Worcestershire sauce
½ cup bread crumbs
4 eggs, separated

Melt butter in saucepan and blend in flour. Add milk and cheese gradually, stirring constantly until thick and smooth.
Add salt, mustard, Worcestershire sauce and bread crumbs.
Mix sauce into chopped ham.
Add beaten egg yolks and let stand to cool.
Preheat oven to 400°.
About 30 minutes before serving time, turn ham mixture into greased 1½-quart souffle dish. Carefully fold in egg whites which have been beaten until stiff.
Bake for 25 minutes or until browned.

4 SERVINGS

Ham Patties with Hollandaise

2 cups ground cooked ham
½ cup long-grain rice (1½ cups cooked)
4 tablespoons cooking oil
¼ cup chopped celery
1 tablespoon chopped green pepper
2 tablespoons chopped onion
2 tablespoons all purpose flour
1 teaspoon dry mustard
½ cup tomato juice
1 beaten egg
1 tablespoon water
½ cup dry bread crumbs
Hollandaise sauce

Combine ground ham and cooked rice.
Cook celery, green pepper and onion in 2 tablespoons oil till tender.

Blend flour and dry mustard into vegetable mixture and add tomato juice. Cook until very thick and bubbly, stirring constantly.

Add to ham mixture and mix well. Chill.

Combine beaten egg and water.

Form ham mixture into 8 patties. Dip in egg mixture, then crumbs.

In skillet, cook patties in remaining 2 tablespoons oil over medium heat until browned.

Serve with warmed Hollandaise sauce mixed with ¼ cup sour cream.

Macaroni and Sausage Casserole

1 pound sausage meat	3 eggs
½ cup chopped onion	1 cup grated sharp Cheddar cheese
1 cup elbow macaroni	
1 can condensed cream of celery soup	¾ cup bread crumbs
⅔ cup milk	1 tablespoon melted butter

Preheat oven to 350°.

Cook sausage and onion until lightly browned. Drain off excess fat.

Cook macaroni according to package directions. Drain.

Combine sausage, macaroni, soup, milk, slightly beaten eggs, and cheese.

Place in 8 x 8 x 2-inch baking dish.

Mix bread crumbs and butter and arrange over casserole.

Bake for 40 minutes.

6 SERVINGS

Bacon-Chicken Bake

8 slices Canadian bacon
8 boned chicken breasts
8 slices bacon
1 can cream of mushroom soup
1 cup sour cream

Preheat oven to 300°.
Place slices of Canadian bacon on bottom of buttered shallow casserole.
Wrap chicken in bacon and place on top of Canadian bacon.
Mix soup and sour cream and pour over the top.
Bake, uncovered, for 2 hours or until done.

6 TO 8 SERVINGS

Sausage and Noodle Bake

3 cups uncooked egg noodles
1 tablespoon salt
1 pound sausage meat
1 can cream of celery soup
1 cup drained sauerkraut
1 cup Cheddar cheese

Cook noodles in salted water.
Saute sausage, drain.
Preheat oven to 350°.
Combine soup, sauerkraut, cheese, cooked noodles and half of sausage. Place in 2-quart casserole. Cover with remaining sausage.
Bake for 30 minutes.

4 SERVINGS

Kidney Beans with Sausage in Wine

3 cans red kidney or pinto beans
2 pounds sausage meat
1 cup finely chopped onion
2 cups red wine
Salt to taste
Freshly ground pepper
6 strips bacon
3 tablespoons chopped parsley

Preheat oven to 350°.
Drain kidney beans in colander and rinse well with cold water.
Make sausage meat into 2-inch cakes.
In shallow skillet put onion, wine, and sausage cakes. Put over medium heat and simmer, covered, for about 30 minutes, until sausage is cooked.
Remove sausage and reduce liquid by half.
Layer sausage cakes and beans in a baking dish and pour reduced liquid over them. Cover with strips of bacon.
Bake for 20 to 30 minutes, until bacon is crisp.
Sprinkle with parsley.

6 SERVINGS

Ham Mousse

3½ cups finely ground ham
1 package gelatin
¼ cup cold water
1⅓ cups chicken bouillon
2 eggs, separated
1 cup cream
¼ cup dry sherry
Watercress for garnish

Soak gelatin in cold water.
Heat chicken bouillon and dissolve gelatin in it.
Beat egg yolks into chicken bouillon and stir over low heat until thickened. Cool.
Stir in sherry.
Beat egg whites until stiff.
Beat cream into soft peaks.
Fold ham, beaten whites, and cream into gelatin mixture. Pour into a mold and chill for several hours.
Unmold and serve garnished with watercress.

6 SERVINGS

Canadian Bacon and Mushroom Pie

2 tablespoons butter or margarine
2 tablespoons flour
1 cup milk
  Salt to taste
  Freshly ground pepper
½ teaspoon nutmeg
2 egg yolks
2 tablespoons cream
3 tablespoons butter or margarine
1 tablespoon chopped shallots or green onions
½ pound mushrooms, sliced
1 cup cooked Canadian bacon, chopped
¼ cup grated Cheddar cheese
8-inch pie shell

Preheat oven to 400°.
In saucepan put 2 tablespoons butter and flour. Cook, stirring, over

high heat for 3 minutes. Add milk and cook, stirring, until thick and smooth. Remove from heat and add seasonings.

Beat yolks and cream together and blend into sauce.

In skillet heat 3 tablespoons butter. Add shallots and mushrooms. Saute until mushrooms are tender, about 10 minutes. Pour off excess liquid.

Sprinkle bacon onto pie shell. Mix sauce and mushrooms together and pour over bacon. Sprinkle with cheese and bake for 15 minutes.

6 SERVINGS

Farmer's Feast

¼ pound sliced bacon
2 small onions, sliced
2 pounds potatoes, cooked and sliced
1 pound sausage, sliced in ½-inch patties.

¼ cup milk
¼ teaspoon salt
2 eggs

Preheat oven to 300°.
Cook sausage.
Fry bacon with onions. Mix in potatoes. In 2-quart casserole alternate layer of potato mixture with layer of sausage patties. Beat milk, salt, and eggs. Pour over layers and bake 30 minutes or until eggs are set.

4 SERVINGS

Turkey Trots

1 pound asparagus spears, cooked 6 slices Cheddar cheese
¼ cup chutney ½ cup milk
½ teaspoon dry mustard Paprika
6 large, thin slices of cooked,
    smoked turkey (or unsmoked)

Preheat oven to 350°.
Roll large slices of smoked turkey around asparagus. Secure with toothpicks.
Place flat in baking dish and lay a slice of cheese over each portion.
Mix chutney and mustard with milk and pour over asparagus.
Sprinkle with paprika.
Bake until the cheese is melted and golden. Serve hot.

6 SERVINGS

Index of Recipes

A

Apple Cake, Dorset, 79
Apple and Ham Pie, 35
Apple Pies, Fried, 99
Apple Tart, Upside-down, 51
Apple Toot, 50
Apples and Onions, Baked, 102
Artichoke, Jerusalem, 61
Asparagus and Ham Casserole, 130
Asparagus in Ambush, 36

B

Bacon, Canadian, and Mushroom Pie, 136
Bacon-Chicken Bake, 134
Bacon, Corn Muffins with, 130
Bacon Dressing, with Spinach Salad, 131
Baked Bean Soup, 94
Baked Beans, 93
Bannock, 70
Barley Vegetable Soup, 56
Barrel Bake, Rhode Island, 39
Bean Pot Stew, 120
Beef, Dried Beef Sauce with Jonnycake, 40
Beef, Dried and Oyster Souffle, 90
Beef and Kidney Pie, 53
Beef Olives, 81
Beef, Spiced, 114
Biscuits, Corner, 8
Biscuits, Soda, 78
Blackstone Pudding, 38
Blueberry Cake, 111
Blueberry Pancakes, 111
Blueberry Pudding, 112
Blueberry Slump, 112
Bluefish, Baked, 110
Boiled Dinner, New England, 101
Braised Shoulder of Lamb, 55
Bread, Bannock, 70
Bread, Portuguese, 63
Bread, Pumpkin, 15
Brown Bread, 54
Buckwheat Cakes, 25
Butter and Sugar Frosting, 125

C

Cabbage Soup, 67
Cake, Black Walnut, 74
Cake, Blueberry, 111
Cake, Dorset Apple, 79
Cake, Honey, 96
Cake, Lobster, 123
Cake, Maple Nut Upside-down, 89
Cake, Newport Spice, 36
Cake, Plum, 24
Cake, Sweet Cream, 125
Cakes, Crab, 29
Cakes, Fried Potato, 76
Cakes, Shrewsbury, 47
Canadian Bacon and Mushroom Pie, 136
Carrot Cookies, 124
Carrot Soup, 95
Carrots and Potatoes, Baked, 52
Cheese and Ham Puff Ring, 129
Cheesecakes, Fried, 104
Chicken-Bacon Bake, 134
Chicken, Boiled with Oyster Sauce, 13
Chicken, or Turkey, Fried, 14

139

Chicken, Scalloped, 100
Chicken Stew, 118
Chicken, Terrapin, 100
Chocolate Puffs, 48
Chowder, Dried Beef, 131
Chowder, Maine Corn, 117
Chowder, Fish, 62
Chowder, Smoked Fish, 122
Cinnamon Maple Toast, 104
Clam Fritters, 20
Clam Pie, 20
Cod, Spicy Salt Cod and Potatoes, 64
Cookies, Carrot, 124
Cookies, Molasses Rounds, 97
Cookies, Snickerdoodles, 124
Corn Chowder, Maine, 117
Corn Muffins with Bacon, 130
Corn Pudding, 76
Corn Pudding, New, 96
Corner Biscuits, 8
Crab Cakes, 29
Crab, Scalloped, 30
Cranberry Pie, Deep-Dish, 60
Cream of Green Pea Soup, 80
Cream, Scorched, 16
Cucumber Sauce with Molded Salmon, 34
Cucumbers, Baked Stuffed, 72
Custard Pie, Maple, 88

D

Deep-Dish Cranberry Pie, 60
Deep-Dish Oyster Pie, 31
Dinner, Farmer's Feast, 137
Dinner, New England Boiled, 101
Dinner, Rhode Island Barrel Bake, 39
Dinner, Six Layer, 21
Doughnuts, 122
Dried Beef and Oyster Souffle, 90
Dried Beef Chowder, 131
Dried Beef Sauce with Jonnycake, 41

E

Eggplant, Planked, 82
Egg Sauce with Salmon, 46
Eggs, Poached in Maple Syrup, 103

F

Farmer's Feast, 137
Fish Chowder, 62
Fish Chowder, Smoked, 122
Flannel Hash, Red, 102
Fried Apple Pies, 99
Fried Cheesecakes, 104
Fried Chicken or Turkey, 14
Fried Potato Cakes, 76
Fried Scallops, 32
Fritters, Clam, 20
Frosting, Butter and Sugar, 125

G

Gingerbread, 46
Goose, Roast, 9
Green Pea Soup, Cream of, 80
Greens, 42

H

Ham and Apple Pie, 35
Ham and Asparagus Casserole, 130
Ham and Cheese Puff Ring, 129
Ham and Veal Pie, 72
Ham Loaf, 92
Ham Mousse, 136
Ham Patties with Hollandaise, 132
Ham Souffle, 132
Hash, Red Flannel, 102
Hedgehog Pudding, 23
Hollandaise, with Ham Patties, 132
Honey Cake, 96

140

I

Indian Pudding, Durgin Park, 48

J

Jerusalem Artichokes, 61
Jonnycake with Dried Beef Sauce, 40

K

Kedgeree, Wakefield, 32
Kidney and Beef Pie, 53
Kidney Beans with Sausage in Wine, 135

L

Lamb, Braised Shoulder of, 55
Layer Dinner, Six, 21
Lima Bean Pudding, 77
Little Boy's Pudding, 39
Lobster Cake, 123
Lobster Stew, 116

M

Macaroni and Sausage Bake, 133
Maple Custard Pie, 88
Maple Nut Upside-down Cake, 89
Maple Syrup, Eggs Poached in, 103
Maple Toast, Cinnamon, 104
Marlborough Pie, 50
Menus, 127
Molasses Rounds, 97
Molasses Sponge, 73
Molasses Taffy, 59
Molded Salmon with Cucumber Sauce, 34
Mousse, Ham, 136
Muffins, Corn, with Bacon, 130
Mushroom and Canadian Bacon Pie, 136
Mussels, Stewed, 113

N

New Corn Pudding, 96
New England Boiled Dinner, 101
Noodle and Sausage Bake, 134

O

Oat Rolls, 68
Oatmeal Scones, 70
Onions and Apples, Baked, 102
Onions, Scalloped, 18
Onion Shortcake, 18
Oyster and Dried Beef Souffle, 90
Oyster Pie, Deep-Dish, 31
Oyster Sauce with Boiled Chicken, 13
Oysters, Panned, 30

P

Pan Dowdy, Peach, 38
Pancakes, Blueberry, 111
Pancakes, Buckwheat, 25
Panned Oysters, 30
Pea Soup, 116
Pea Soup, Cream of Green, 80
Peach Pan Dowdy, 38
Pie, Beef and Kidney, 53
Pie, Canadian Bacon and Mushroom, 136
Pie, Clam, 20
Pie, Cranberry Deep-Dish, 60
Pie, Fried Apple, 99
Pie, Ham and Apple, 35
Pie, Maple Custard, 88
Pie, Marlborough, 50
Pie, Oyster, Deep-Dish, 31
Pie, Rabbit, 121
Pie, Rhubarb, 109
Pie, Shoofly, 82
Pie, Veal and Ham, 72
Pie, Washington, 69
Planked Eggplant, 82

Plum Cake, 24
Portuguese Bread, 63
Pot Stew, Bean, 120
Potato Cakes, Fried, 76
Potatoes and Carrots, Baked, 52
Potatoes and Spicy Salt Cod, 64
Pudding, Apple Toot, 50
Pudding, Blackstone, 38
Pudding, Blueberry, 112
Pudding, Connecticut Peach, 22
Pudding, Corn, 76
Pudding, Cranberry Deep-Dish, 60
Pudding, Hedgehog, 23
Pudding, Indian, Durgin Park, 48
Pudding, Lima Bean, 77
Pudding, Little Boy's, 39
Pudding, New Corn, 96
Pudding, Pumpkin, 16, 98
Pudding, Sausage, 91
Puffs, Chocolate, 48
Pumpkin Bread, 15
Pumpkin Pudding, 16, 98

R

Rabbit Pie, 121
Red Flannel Hash, 102
Rhode Island Barrel Bake, 39
Rhubarb Pie, 109
Roast Goose, 9
Rolls, Oat, 68

S

Salad, Mess O' Greens, 42
Salad, Spinach, with Bacon Dressing, 131
Salmon with Egg Sauce, 46
Salmon, Molded with Cucumber Sauce, 34
Sauce, Cucumber with Molded Salmon, 34
Sauce, Dried Beef with Jonnycake, 40
Sauce, Egg with Salmon, 46
Sauce for Goose, 9

Sauce, Oyster with Boiled Chicken, 13
Sausage and Macaroni Bake, 133
Sausage and Noodle Bake, 134
Sausage Pudding, 91
Sausage with Kidney Beans in Wine, 135
Scalloped Chicken, 100
Scalloped Crab, 30
Scalloped Onions, 18
Scallops, Sauteed, 118
Scallops, Fried, 32
Scones, Oatmeal, 70
Scorched Cream, 16
Shad, Baked, 57
Shad Roe, 57
Shoofly Pie, 82
Shortcake, Onion, 18
Shrewsbury Cakes, 47
Shrimp Soup, 115
Six Layer Dinner, 21
Slump, Blueberry, 112
Smelts, Maine Baked, 114
Smoked Fish Chowder, 122
Snickerdoodles, 124
Soda Biscuits, 78
Souffle, Dried Beef and Oyster, 90
Souffle, Ham, 132
Souffle, Molasses Sponge, 73
Soup, Baked Bean, 94
Soup, Barley Vegetable, 56
Soup, Cabbage, 67
Soup, Carrot, 95
Soup, Cream of Green Pea, 80
Soup, Pea, 116
Soup, Shrimp, 115
Spareribs, Baked, 58
Spice Cake, Newport, 36
Spicy Salt Cod and Potatoes, 64
Spinach Salad with Bacon Dressing, 131
Sponge, Molasses, 73
Stew, Bean Pot, 120
Stew, Chicken, 118
Stew, Lobster, 116

Stewed Mussels, 113
Sweet Cream Cake, 125

T

Taffy, Molasses, 59
Tart, Upside-down Apple, 51
Terrapin Chicken, 100
Toast, Cinnamon Maple, 104
Trout, Grilled, 75
Turkey or Chicken, Fried, 14
Turkey Trots, 138

U

Upside-down Apple Tart, 51
Upside-down Cake, Maple Nut, 89

V

Veal and Ham Pie, 72
Vegetable Barley Soup, 56

W

Wakefield Kedgeree, 32
Walnut Cake, Black, 74
Washington Pie, 69
Wine, Kidney Beans and Sausage in, 135